José María   Iba
     ell
     z

Jon Hird

Sue Kay

Elisa Jiménez Lazcano

Peter Maggs

Carmen Santos Maldonado

Fernando Martín Pescador

Nicholas Sheard

Inside Out

Resource Pack

Elementary

MACMILLAN

Macmillan Education
Between Towns Road, Oxford OX4 3PP
A division of Macmillan Publishers Limited
Companies and representatives throughout the world

ISBN 0 333 97582 0

First published 2004

Designed by Anthony Godber
Illustrations by Kathy Baxendale worksheets 0, 1A, 2B, 6A, 6B,
13A; Mark Draisey worksheets 3B, 4A, 9B, 11A, 19A;
Bill Piggins worksheets 8B, 18A
Cover design by Andrew Oliver

Printed and bound in Great Britain
by Martins the Printers Ltd, Berwick upon Tweed

2008 2007 2006 2005 2004
10 9 8 7 6 5 4 3

Introduction

This Resource Pack for teachers contains thirty-seven practice activities for Elementary students of English. It is designed to be used with *Inside Out* Elementary Student's Book.

Ten practising teachers have contributed activities, so you'll find a wealth of different ideas for practising skills and specific language points. All the activities have been tested in the classroom.

Using the worksheets

You can use the activities in many different ways. For example:

- to extend the lessons in the Student's Book
- as revision of points in the Student's Book, for example at the beginning of the following lesson
- to supplement other courses
- as a basis for standby lessons.

How to use the Resource Pack

Each activity consists of one photocopiable worksheet original. The originals have been designed for maximum clarity when photocopied. However, if your photocopier has the facility to enlarge, you may sometimes find this useful – particularly for board games or worksheets which are to be cut up into cards.

Each original appears on the right-hand page, with teacher's notes on the left-hand page so that you can see them both at the same time. The notes explain the aims of the activity, describe the task, tell you what you need to do to prepare and then give a step-by-step lesson plan, This makes them easy to use if you haven't been teaching long, but it is also a terrific time-saver for experienced teachers. Regard the lesson plans as a starting point. As you use the worksheets you'll find your own ways of making the best of them in class. Some of the worksheets need cutting up into sections. To make these easier to handle in the classroom, glue them onto small pieces of card – index cards or blank business cards, available from most stationers, are ideal. After the lesson, file the cards in an envelope for the next time you use them. Write the name of the activity and the number of cards on the outside.

Some activities require multiple sets of cards. In these cases, it is a good idea to distinguish each set in some way. Put a different mark, preferably in different coloured pens, on the cards from each set. Or, even better, photocopy them on different coloured papers. This will save you time when you re-file them at the end of the lesson.

Over to you

If you have any comments about *Inside Out*, you will find a feedback form on our website at www.insideout.net, where you can also register to receive extra teaching materials free every week by e-mail. Your opinions will help to shape our future publishing.

Contents

Worksheet	Timing	Task	Aim (lexis, grammar, pronunciation, skills)
10 *Stop!*	10–15 minutes	To match questions and answers.	To consolidate the main language areas covered in Units 1 to 9 of *Inside Out* Elementary Student's Book.
11A *Fashion and style*	20 minutes	To match words for clothes and accessories with two pictures (one of a woman and the other of a man).	To revise vocabulary related to clothes and accessories and practise using the present continuous.
11B *Match the numbers*	10 minutes	To play a game of matching pairs (pelmanism).	To practise saying numbers (13/30, 14/40 etc.)
12A *Who am I?*	15–20 minutes	To ask questions to identify the other student.	To practise the use of the forms: *want to, would like to, hope to, going to.*
12B *Make a sentence with …*	10–15 minutes	To make sentences using the verbs on two cards (pelmanism).	To practise making sentences using verb patterns starting with *want to, would like to, hope to* and *going to.*
13A *What is it?*	15–30 minutes	To guess the identity of an object by asking *Yes/No* questions.	To consolidate and further practise language for describing objects.
13B *Quiz time*	30 minutes	To complete a quiz by ordering three items according to size etc.	To consolidate and practise comparatives and superlatives.
14A *What should I do?*	15–30 minutes	To guess a situation by using the advice/clues from different classmates.	To practise vocabulary related to problems and giving advice (*should/shouldn't*).
14B *Character jumble*	20–30 minutes	To complete a crossword by rearranging the jumbled letters of character adjectives and then to discuss questions about the adjectives.	To consolidate and practise adjectives of character.
15 *Silly mistakes*	20–30 minutes	To correct mistakes in fourteen sentences and then to use these sentences for discussion.	To consolidate and further practise the main language areas covered in units 11 to 15 of *Inside Out* Elementary Student's Book.
16A *The internet and me*	25–35 minutes	To dictate a text to a partner, and then ask and answer questions in groups.	To practise present perfect questions about the internet.
16B *Have you ever bingo*	20–30 minutes	To complete a bingo card with students' names by asking questions.	To consolidate and practise present perfect + *ever*.
17A *Circuit training*	40–50 minutes	To work in groups and complete a worksheet.	To revise and practise structures, vocabulary and pronunciation introduced in *Inside Out* Elementary Student's Book.
17B *It takes ages!*	15–20 minutes	To mill around the classroom, asking and answering questions.	To practise questions about transport to work or school.
18A *How do you do it?*	10–15 minutes	To mime an action to a group who try to guess the action and the adverb of manner.	To practise adverbs of manner.
18B *Telling tales*	20–30 minutes	To put the different parts of a story into the correct order. To create an ending for the story.	To practise reading skills and to use time adverbials in context.
19A *Find someone*	20 minutes	To make some questions and then ask other students in the class to answer them.	To practise making questions using the passive.
19B *Weather forecast*	40 minutes	To present a weather forecast.	To practise using *will* and *might*.
20 *Jeopardy*	30–40 minutes	To choose and answer a variety of questions covering grammar, vocabulary, pronunciation and speaking skills.	To consolidate some of the grammar, vocabulary and pronunciation covered in *Inside Out* Elementary Student's Book.

0 *Classroom crossword*

Sue Kay

Type of activity

Information-gap crossword. Pair work.

Aim

To practise vocabulary related to the classroom.

Task

To complete the gaps in a crossword by asking a partner to point at pictures that represent the missing words.

Preparation

Make one copy of the worksheet for each pair and cut the copies up as indicated.

Timing

20–25 minutes.

Procedure

1 Draw a simple crossword on the board and pre-teach the following words: *crossword, clue, across, down.*

2 Put the students into pairs and explain that you are going to give everybody the same crossword, but that Student A has the down words already written in, and Student B has the across words already written in.

3 Give a copy of Crossword A and Clues A to each Student A and a copy of Crossword B and Clues B to each Student B.

4 Explain that they must not show their crossword to their partner.

5 Ask them to sit facing one another and to take it in turns to ask their partner for clues to the missing words, for example:
Student A: *What is 4 across?*
Student B: *(points to the picture of a teacher) This.*
(Student A writes 'teacher' in the space.)

Answers

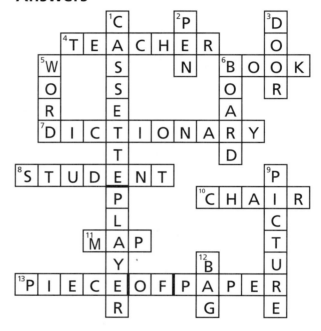

Follow-up

Cut up one set of pictures per pair of students and stick each picture onto a piece of paper. Write the answers on pieces of paper the same size as the pictures, so that each pair of students has one set of pictures and one set of words. Students can then place all the pieces of paper face down on their desks and play pelmanism, trying to match the correct pictures and words.

0 *Classroom crossword*

Crossword A

Ask your partner for clues to find the missing words.

Clues A

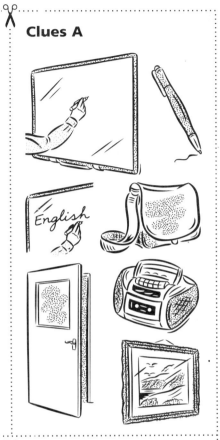

Crossword B

Ask your partner for clues to find the missing words.

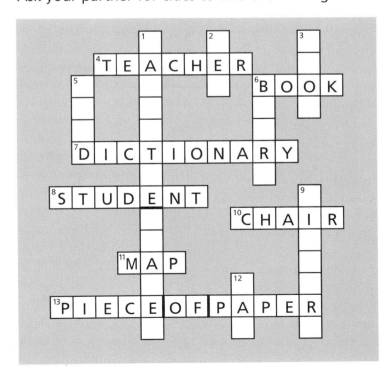

Clues B

Photocopiable

1A *True or false?*

Sue Kay

Type of activity

Pair work. Speaking.

Aim

To practise talking about favourites.

Task

To write true and false sentences about the students' favourite things and to guess a partner's true and false sentences.

Preparation

Make one copy of the worksheet for each student.

Timing

15–20 minutes.

Procedure

1 Write three sentences about your own favourite things on the board. For example:
   My favourite food is potatoes.
   My favourite drink is apple juice.
   My favourite sport is baseball.
   Two sentences should be true and the other one false.

2 Explain to the students the meaning of *true* and *false* and ask them to guess which of your sentences is the false one.

3 Encourage the students to ask the question *Is your favourite drink apple juice?* and answer *Yes, it is.* or *No, it isn't.*

4 Now ask the students to work in pairs and give one copy of the worksheet to each student.

5 Tell the students that they are going to write true and false sentences about their own favourite things and then guess whether their partner's sentences are true or false.

6 Ask them to complete the ten sentences on the worksheet with a mixture of true and false information. You can tell them how many sentences to make true and how many to make false if you like.

7 When they have done that, ask them to exchange worksheets with their partner. They should read their partner's sentences and put a *T* next to sentences they think are true and an *F* next to those they think are false. Pairs of students should not speak to one another during this part of the activity.

8 When they have finished, students take it in turns to ask their partners questions to find out whether they have guessed correctly or not. Encourage them to use the target language. They should keep a record of how many sentences they guessed correctly and write the score at the bottom of their partner's worksheet. The student with the most correct guesses is the winner.

1A *True or false?*

Complete these sentences about your favourite things. Make some sentences true and some sentences false.

Exchange worksheets with your partner. Can you guess the false sentences?

My favourite food is _____

My favourite drink is _____

My favourite car is _____

My favourite sport is _____

My favourite actor is _____

My favourite singer is _____

My favourite day of the week is _____

My favourite month is _____

My favourite city is _____

Photocopiable

1B Can you spell that?

Jon Hird

Type of activity

Information exchange.

Aims

To consolidate and practise pronunciation of the letters of the alphabet and telephone numbers.

Task

To ask for and give information to spell names, addresses, email addresses and telephone numbers.

Preparation

Make one copy of the worksheet for each pair of students and cut in half where indicated.

Timing

15–30 minutes.

Procedure

1 Put the students into pairs and give worksheet A to one student from each pair and worksheet B to the other student.

2 Tell the students they must 'phone' their partner to ask them for the missing information so that they can complete their address books. Students should sit back to back so that they cannot see each other.

3 When all the information has been exchanged, the students can check by looking at the original versions.

Follow up

The students can exchange their own real-life personal details (name, address, email address, phone number) with their partner and then write an email (real or on paper) to their partner to thank them for the help they gave them earlier.

Notes & comments

Monitor and note down any letter pronunciation that needs reviewing.

1B *Can you spell that?*

A

You have deleted some address files on your computer by mistake. Phone your friend and ask him or her for the missing information.

Have you got May's/his/her address/email address/phone number?
Can you spell that?
Could you repeat that?

| @ = at | . = dot |
| _ = underscore | .com = dot com |

First name: **Mariela Ana**
Last name: **Mazzei**
Nickname: **Mazzy**
Address: **Av. Brasil 1764, Montevideo, Uruguay**
Email address: **m_mazzei@arnet.com.uy**
Phone number: **709 8944**

First name: _____
Last name: _____
Nickname: **May** _____
Address: _____
_____
Email address: _____
Phone number: _____

First name: **Kwanchai**
Last name: **Suphaphong**
Nickname: **Kwan**
Address: **134 Sri Ayutha Road, Soi 32, Si Sou Tewet, Bangkok, Thailand**
Email address: **kwansup@hotmail.com**
Phone number: **02 281 2475**

First name: _____
Last name: _____
Nickname: **Franc** _____
Address: _____
_____
Email address: _____
Phone number: _____

B

You have deleted some address files on your computer by mistake. Phone your friend and ask him or her for the missing information.

Have you got Mazzy's/his/her address/email address/phone number?
Can you spell that?
Could you repeat that?

| @ = at | . = dot |
| _ = underscore | .com = dot com |

First name: **Mayumi**
Last name: **Oyake**
Nickname: **May**
Address: **45 Sanae-cho, Nishi-ku, Nagoya, Japan**
Email address: **m.oyake22@hotmail.com**
Phone number: **052 451 9830**

First name: _____
Last name: _____
Nickname: **Mazzy** _____
Address: _____
_____
Email address: _____
Phone number: _____

First name: **Francois**
Last name: **Amilhat**
Nickname: **Franc**
Address: **13a Boulevard Victor, 75016, Paris, France**
Email address: **f_amilhat6@compuserve.com**
Phone number: **66 304 12 77**

First name: _____
Last name: _____
Nickname: **Kwan** _____
Address: _____
_____
Email address: _____
Phone number: _____

Photocopiable

2A *Family photos*

Sue Kay

Type of activity

Group work. Speaking.

Aim

To practise family vocabulary and giving personal details.

Task

To show photos of real or invented members of the family and talk about them.

Preparation

Make one copy of the worksheet for each student. Cut out pictures from magazines of different groups of between two and five people – at least one picture per group of three or four students.

Timing

30–40 minutes.

Procedure

1 Ask the students to work in small groups of three or four and give each group a picture cut out from a magazine (see *Preparation*).

2 Tell the students that they have to imagine that these are photographs of members of their own family, and that in a moment they are going to talk to their partners about them.

3 Give one copy of the worksheet to each student and ask them to invent identities for the people in the photograph by writing answers to the questions on the worksheet. Give them the time they need to do this, and be on hand to help them with the language they need.

4 When the students have done this, ask them to take it in turns to show the picture to the other students in their group, and explain who the people in the photograph are.

Follow up

Ask the students to bring photographs of real members of their family to class and do the same activity.

Notes & comments

You may like to demonstrate the activity before asking the students to do it. Choose a picture from a magazine and hold it up in front of the class. Go round the class asking students to invent personal information for the person in the picture. Each student has to repeat the information already invented by other students and then add another piece of information themselves.

2A *Family photos*

Write about your family.

Names: _____

_____

_____

What relation are they to you?

_____

_____

_____

How old are they? _____

_____

_____

Where do they live? _____

What do they do? _____

_____

Are they married or single? _____

_____

Have they got any children? _____

_____

When do you see them? _____

_____

Other information _____

_____

_____

Attach photo here

Photocopiable

2B Where in the world?

Jon Hird

Type of activity

Board game.

Aims

To consolidate and further practise countries, nationalities and languages.

Task

To play a board game by saying the names of countries, nationalities and languages and by answering general knowledge questions.

Preparation

Make one copy of the worksheet for every group of two to four students (this could be enlarged to A3 size if possible). You may also want to give each student a copy of the worksheet at the end of the activity.

Each group will need one dice. If you do not have any dice, the students could use a coin; for 'heads' move one square forward and 'tails' move two squares forward.

Each student will need one counter.

Timing

20–30 minutes.

Procedure

1 Put your students into groups of two to four and give each group a worksheet, a dice and one counter per student.

2 Tell the students they are going to play a board game and explain the rules as follows:

a Start on the DEPARTURES square. Roll the dice and move around the board as follows: If you land on a:

map, give the *country and the nationality.*
flag, give the *country and the language.*
famous building, give the *country and the capital city.*
question, choose the *correct answer.*
'Miss a turn' square, *miss your next turn.*
There is a reminder of this on the board game.

b If the answer is correct, you can play the next turn. If it is incorrect, go back to the last 'Miss a turn' square and miss the next turn. The other students should decide if the answer is correct or not, including the word stress. Ask the teacher if you are not sure of the correct answer.

c The winner is the first person to reach the ARRIVALS square.

Answers

1
2 The United Kingdom, British
3 France, Paris
4 Italy, Italian
5
6 Egypt, Cairo
7 China
8 Saudi Arabia, Arabic
9 Russia, Moscow
10
11 India, Indian
12 190 (but this may change from time to time)
13 China, Chinese (mainly Mandarin or Cantonese)
14 Japan, Japanese
15
16 Thailand, Thai
17 Asia
18 Australia, Canberra
19
20 South Africa, English and Afrikaans
21 Argentina, Spanish
22 6-7 billion (estimates are: year 2000 – 6.2 billion, 2005 – 6.4 billion, 2010 – 6.8 billion, 2020 – 7.8 billion)
23 Brazil, Portuguese
24 The United States of America, American

Follow up

You could run through each country and check the country, nationality and language for each. Also check the word stress.

2B *Where in the world?*

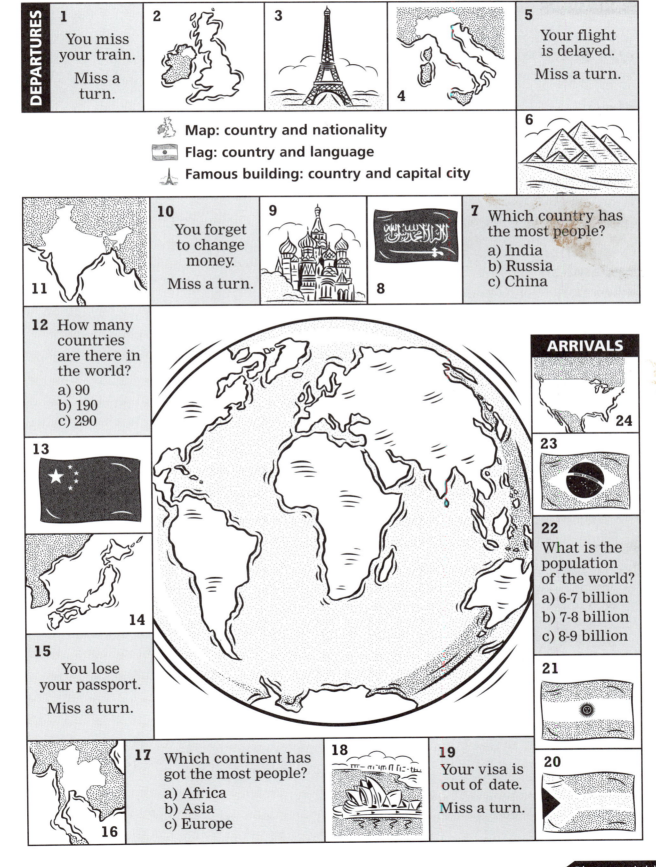

DEPARTURES

1 You miss your train. Miss a turn.

2

3

4

5 Your flight is delayed. Miss a turn.

Map: country and nationality
Flag: country and language
Famous building: country and capital city

6

10 You forget to change money. Miss a turn.

9

8

7 Which country has the most people?
a) India
b) Russia
c) China

11

12 How many countries are there in the world?
a) 90
b) 190
c) 290

13

14

15 You lose your passport. Miss a turn.

16

17 Which continent has got the most people?
a) Africa
b) Asia
c) Europe

18

19 Your visa is out of date. Miss a turn.

20

21

22 What is the population of the world?
a) 6-7 billion
b) 7-8 billion
c) 8-9 billion

23

ARRIVALS

24

Photocopiable

3A *I love playing charades!*

Carmen Santos Maldonado

Type of activity

Grammar and vocabulary. Speaking. Group work.

Aims

To practise word order. To practise vocabulary of likes and dislikes, and daily activities.

Task

To guess the exact wording of sentences mimed by other students.

Preparation

Make one copy of the worksheet and cut it up as indicated.

Timing

15–20 minutes.

Procedure

1   Tell your students that they are going to guess the exact words of sentences being mimed to them. Explain that all the sentences are statements about likes and dislikes and daily activities.

2   Demonstrate the activity yourself by miming the example sentences (below) to the whole class and asking the students to call out words to describe what you are doing. Use any gestures or point to any object in the classroom (a calendar, your watch, colours ...) to make yourself understood. Indicate *yes* or *no* with your head, to direct the students, but do not say a word or draw anything on the board. As the students guess the right words, write them on the board. Example sentences:
I like getting up late on Sundays.
I hate playing computer games.

3   Divide the class into two teams (A and B). Place the cut-out sentences, face down, on your desk. Tell each team to send one player to the front of the class. The players each pick up one sentence and read it. They must then mime the sentence for their own team. They will have one minute per sentence. Explain that they can use any gestures or point to any object in the classroom to help their team guess the words.

4   One of the other team members must write the sentence on the board as their team guesses the words.

5   Students in each team then take it in turns to mime a sentence until all the sentences have been mimed. Then read out the correct sentences to the whole class and ask the teams to add up their score according to scale below.

Exact sentence: 3 points
One mistake: 2 points
Two mistakes: 1 point
Three mistakes or more: 0 points

Follow up

Ask students to write six 'mimable' sentences about a member of their family, explaining his/her daily routines and likes and dislikes.

Notes & comments

This game can also be played in pairs. Each player has half the sentences. Students take it in turns to mime to each other; if their partner guesses correctly, they get the sentences. The winner is the player with the most sentences at the end.

3A *I love playing charades!*

I love skiing in winter.

I don't like writing letters.

I like playing the guitar in the evenings.

I don't mind doing the washing up.

I like reading the newspaper after breakfast.

I hate watching football on TV.

I love listening to very loud music in the car.

I hate ironing trousers.

I don't like getting up before 10 am on Sundays.

I really like going to the beach in summer.

I love reading fashion magazines.

I don't mind Chinese food.

Photocopiable

3B Daily life

Elisa Jiménez Lazcano

Type of activity

Writing and speaking. Individual and pair work.

Aims

To practise question forms, and revise the present simple and adverbs of frequency.

Task

To exchange information about someone and complete a text with this information.

Preparation

Make one copy of the worksheet for each pair and cut the copies up as indicated.

Timing

20 minutes.

Procedure

1   Divide the class into two groups, group A and group B. Give each student in group A a copy of the Student A worksheet and each student in group B a copy of the Student B worksheet.

2   Ask students in their groups to read through the question prompts and write out the full questions by inserting *do* or *does*.

3   Put the students into A / B pairs and explain that they have the same text about Herbert and Shirley but that some information is missing. Allow a minute or two for students to read through their texts.

4   Explain that students have to complete the text by asking their partner the questions given in each worksheet. Students should take it in turns to ask and answer their questions.

5   Check the answers with the whole class.

Follow up

Students can practise speaking about their own daily life by asking each other similar questions to those on the worksheets.

Write other prompts on the board so that students can make more questions in the present simple.
What/do in the afternoon?
What/phone number?
Where/work (study)?
What sports/play?
What kind of music/like?
What TV programmes/like?
What books/magazines/read?
What/like doing at weekends?

Notes & comments

You might want to pre-teach the expression *look like ...* before asking students to read the text, to ensure that there is no confusion between *look like* and *like + ing*.

3B *Daily life*

Student A

Read the text below about Herbert and Shirley. Then use these prompts to ask Student B questions in order to complete the text.

1 What / he do?
2 / he ever get up early?
3 What / he eat for breakfast?
4 What / he do after breakfast?
5 Where / Herbert and Shirley have lunch?
6 / Herbert and Shirley like shopping?
7 How many nightclubs / they go to every night?

Herbert is a (1) _____ . He looks like David Beckham. He always gets up (2) _____ , about 10 a.m. and goes for a run. Then he has (3) _____ for breakfast and (4) _____ . Sometimes he opens new shopping malls or sports centres. He often works with his friend, Shirley, who looks like Victoria Beckham. They usually eat lunch at a (5) _____ at about 1.30. The restaurant pays them to eat there. Lots of people come into the restaurant and look at them. They don't mind. Herbert and Shirley (6) _____ . They read about David and Victoria's clothes and then buy similar clothes. They often visit the hairdresser and change their hairstyles to match David and Victoria's. Herbert has dinner at home, but he is very busy in the evening. He goes to (7) _____ nightclubs every night. He doesn't have to pay – the nightclubs pay him. Everyone wants to go to the clubs and see 'David Beckham'. He usually gets home at about 3 in the morning. Herbert loves his job. 'I'm David Beckham's biggest fan!' he says.

Student B

Read the text below about Herbert and Shirley. Then use these prompts to ask Student A questions in order to complete the text.

1 What time / Herbert get up?
2 What / he do before breakfast?
3 What / he open?
4 When / Herbert and Shirley have lunch?
5 / Herbert and Shirley often go to the hairdresser?
6 Where / Herbert have dinner?
7 What time / Herbert get home?

Herbert is a 'lookalike'. He looks like David Beckham. He always gets up late, about (1) _____ and (2) _____. Then he has bacon and eggs for breakfast and phones his agent. Sometimes he opens (3) _____ or sports centres. He often works with his friend, Shirley, who looks like Victoria Beckham. They usually eat lunch at a French restaurant at about (4) _____ . The restaurant pays them to eat there. Lots of people come into the restaurant and look at them. They don't mind. Herbert and Shirley love shopping. They read about David and Victoria's clothes and then buy similar clothes. They (5) _____ go to the hairdresser and change their hairstyles to match David and Victoria's. Herbert has (6) _____ , but he is very busy in the evening. He goes to three or four nightclubs every night. He doesn't have to pay – the nightclubs pay him. Everyone wants to go to the clubs and see 'David Beckham'. He usually gets home at about (7) _____ in the morning. Herbert loves his job. 'I'm David Beckham's biggest fan!' he says.

Photocopiable

4A *In my room...*

Philip Borrell

Type of activity
Speaking. Small groups.

Aim
To practise the use of *there is/are*, furniture and prepositions of place.

Task
To guess a room from a student's description.

Preparation
Make one OHT copy of the worksheet, or make one copy of the worksheet for each student.

Make one copy of the worksheet for each group of three or four students, and cut the copies up as indicated.

(Variation 1: only the OHT or one copy of the worksheet for each student is needed.)

(Variation 2: make one copy of the worksheet for each student.)

Timing
15–25 minutes.

Procedure
1 Put on the OHT of the worksheet or give one copy of the worksheet to each student, and elicit sentences about picture 1.
2 Ask the students: *Which room is mine?* and describe one of the pictures until a student guesses correctly. Repeat this one or two times.
3 Now ask a student in the class to do the same. Repeat a few times.
4 Demonstrate the activity with two or three strong students. Place a set of the picture cards face down on the table. One student picks up the top card and describes the room on that card. The other students listen and guess the room number (each student has only one guess per card). The first student to say the correct room wins the card for one point. Then the next student picks up a card, describes it, and so on.

5 Divide the students into groups of three to four and give out one set of cards per group.
6 Students play the game in their groups. Monitor closely and feed in ideas where necessary.

Variation 1
1 Put on the OHT of the worksheet or give one copy of the worksheet to each student.
2 Ask a student to choose a room and then you ask various *yes / no* questions to try to find out which room it is. Use *Is there a … ?* and *Are there any … ?* questions. Write notes on the board as the student answers your questions, e.g.: *one coffee table, no lamp* etc. Encourage other students to ask questions as well.
3 Demonstrate the game again, this time with students asking questions, in turn, around the classroom. Note that in this version, a student can only guess which room it is *after* they ask their question.
4 Students then play the game in pairs or small groups.

Variation 2
1 Give out one worksheet to each student.
2 Seat the students in two lines of chairs facing each other, with students directly opposite each other as pairs. One student in each pair then describes a picture until his/her partner guesses the room. After a few minutes of this, students stand and move one chair in a clockwise direction to get a new partner. Do this three or four times.

4A *In my room…*

Photocopiable

4B Ready, steady, search

Jon Hird

Type of activity

Wordsearch. Pair work.

Aim

To consolidate and further practise opposite adjectives.

Task

To work in pairs and each complete a wordsearch. To match opposite adjectives.

Preparation

Make one copy of the worksheet for each pair and cut the copies up as indicated.

Timing

15–30 minutes.

Procedure

1 Put the students into pairs and give one the Student A worksheet and the other the Student B worksheet.
2 Ask the students to find eight more adjectives in their wordsearch puzzle, circling the words and writing them in the 'My words' column of the table as they find them.
3 When they have done this, students A and B work together, exchanging their adjectives to complete the table.

Follow up

Ask the students, working in pairs, to produce some true sentences, either written or spoken, using the pairs of opposite adjectives. For example: *The school is old, but the classrooms are modern. We think tennis is wonderful, but football is awful.*

Answers

warm / cold
clean / dirty
happy / miserable
wonderful / awful
tidy / untidy

cheap / expensive
modern / old
dry / wet
friendly / unfriendly
light / dark

A

B

Notes & comments

1 The 'filler' letters are all consonants and all the vowels are therefore part of an adjective. If needed, you can help the students by telling them to locate the vowels as a starting point for each word.
2 If you think it appropriate for your class, the activity can be done as a race with the first pair successfully to complete the table being the winners.

4B *Ready, steady, search*

A

1 Find eight more adjectives and write them in the 'My words' column.
Five words go across ➡, four words go down ⬇ and one word goes diagonally ⬊.

C	H	E	A	P	S	H	R	W	J
K	G	K	R	M	C	A	D	O	W
C	B	Q	X	O	Z	P	C	N	S
W	L	J	B	D	Y	P	G	D	G
Y	T	E	V	E	S	Y	H	E	T
K	D	K	A	R	N	W	A	R	M
F	R	I	E	N	D	L	Y	F	J
M	Y	R	D	Z	P	V	H	U	M
T	I	D	Y	L	W	L	J	L	B
X	L	I	G	H	T	S	G	C	M

MY WORDS	OPPOSITES
warm	
wonderful	

2 Work with student B and complete the table with his/her words to make ten pairs of opposites.

B

1 Find eight more adjectives and write them in the 'My words' column.
Five words go across ➡, four words go down ⬇ and one word goes diagonally ⬊.

X	O	L	D	R	E	P	K	Q	S
F	D	Y	T	G	X	T	F	T	F
Y	P	A	W	T	P	N	K	L	X
U	N	F	R	I	E	N	D	L	Y
N	S	G	B	K	N	Z	Y	A	D
T	H	P	W	N	S	W	F	W	J
I	X	C	E	M	I	P	D	F	R
D	I	R	T	Y	V	C	K	U	G
Y	R	Y	B	K	E	C	O	L	D
M	I	S	E	R	A	B	L	E	T

MY WORDS	OPPOSITES
cold	
awful	

2 Work with student A and complete the table with his/her words to make ten pairs of opposites.

Photocopiable

5 Identical twins?

Carmen Santos Maldonado

Type of activity
Reading and speaking. Individual and pair work.

Aim
To practise 3rd person 's', adverbs of frequency, like + -ing, questions and short answers. To revise appearance, daily routines, likes and dislikes.

Task
To read a text and communicate to find differences.

Preparation
Make a copy of the worksheet for each pair and cut the copies up as indicated.

Timing
25-30 minutes.

Procedure
1 Introduce the characters in the text to the students. Explain that Mary-Jo and Emma are twin sisters. They now lead quite different lives, and therefore there are some differences between them, as well as similarities. Tell the students that they are going to read an account of what they are like now.
2 Write the following words on the board: age, hair and eyes, house, job, favourite colour, married, sports, pets, holidays. Ask the students to predict in what areas Mary-Jo and Emma are still likely to be similar and in what areas they are more likely to be different.
3 Put the students into pairs and explain that Student A will read about Mary-Jo and Student B will read about Emma. They have to find out how different the two sisters are now.
4 Pre-teach: glasses, paragliding, ice skating, courier.
5 Give worksheet A to each Student A and worksheet B to each Student B. Allow 5-8 minutes for silent reading. Circulate, helping with vocabulary and making sure students do not look at each other's text.

6 Explain to the students that they have to find at least eight differences between Mary-Jo and Emma by sharing their information and asking each other questions, for example: What's Emma's favourite colour? Are Mary-Jo's eyes green? How often does Emma visit her parents?
7 Check the differences with the whole class. There are 12 differences altogether.

Follow up
Ask all the pairs (or early-finishers) to find six similarities between Mary-Jo and Emma.

Notes & comments
If you want to introduce a competitive element to the game, you can set a time limit of 10 minutes and ask the students to try to find as many differences as possible in that time.

Answers
Differences

Mary-Jo:	Emma:
• long black hair	• short fair hair

• left eye: green
  right eye: blue
	• left eye: blue
	  right eye: green

• glasses	• contact lenses
• not married	• married
• pilot	• musician & courier
• good pay	• not good pay

• has a baby snake &
  a parrot
	• has a big dog &
	  a rabbit

• lives in a flat
  in the city
	• lives in a house outside
	  the city

• no garden	• garden

• visits parents every
  week
	• visits parents Christmas &
	  summer

• goes ice skating	• goes skiing & snowboarding
• plays tennis well	• plays tennis badly

Similarities
Both:

• 29 years old	• each eye is a different colour
• tall & pretty	• favourite colour is blue
• love their animals	• go paragliding

5 *Identical twins?*

Student A

Read this text about Mary-Jo. Then ask your partner questions to find out about Mary-Jo's twin, Emma. How many differences can you find between the twins?

Mary-Jo is very good-looking. She's tall, with long black hair. Her eyes are quite unusual because they're a different colour: her left eye is green and her right eye is blue. She wears bright blue-green glasses.

Mary-Jo is 29. She's not married but she's got a lot of admirers!

She is a pilot, so she often spends long periods away from home. She likes her job very much: the salary is good and she has plenty of free time for her favourite sports, paragliding in the Scottish mountains in summer, and ice skating in winter.

She lives in a small flat in the centre of town, so she doesn't have a garden. However, she loves animals and she has two exotic pets, a baby snake and a blue parrot.

Mary-Jo enjoys shopping but she never goes shopping at weekends because the shops are too busy. She loves buying clothes and often buys three or four items in her favourite colour, blue! On Saturday afternoons she visits her parents, out in the country, and on Sunday mornings she usually plays tennis with her twin sister Emma. She loves this because she always wins the match!

Student B

Read this text about Emma. Then ask your partner questions to find out about Emma's twin, Mary-Jo. How many differences can you find between the twins?

Emma and her husband are musicians. They work for a small record label. The pay isn't very good, so Emma also has a part-time job as a motorbike courier. She works in the evenings and at weekends. Her motorbike is new and is in her favourite colour, blue.

Emma is nearly 30. She is very pretty. She's tall with short, fair hair. Her eyes are very unusual: they are a different colour. Her left eye is blue and her right eye is green. She hates glasses, so she wears contact lenses

Emma and her husband have two children. They live in a small house outside the city. They have a lovely garden with a few trees. She loves animals and she has a big dog and a rabbit. She can only visit her parents at Christmas and in summer because she lives very far away from them.

She likes spending her winter holidays skiing and snowboarding in the mountains. In the summer, she enjoys paragliding with her twin sister Mary-Jo. On Sunday mornings she often plays tennis with Mary-Jo. She's not very good at tennis and she always loses. She hates losing!

Photocopiable

6A Containers

Peter Maggs

Type of activity

Matching and speaking. Individual or pair work.

Aim

To practise names of containers.

Task

To match a container with its contents and then play a memory game.

Preparation

Make one copy of the worksheet for each student.

Timing

15 minutes.

Procedure

1 Give a copy of the worksheet to each student in the class.

2 Ask students to fold their piece of paper in half and look at the pictures in the bottom half. Tell them to write the name of the item next to each picture, for example, *lemonade* next to the bottle of lemonade. When students have finished writing, ask them to compare answers with a partner.

3 Ask students to unfold their pieces of paper and work with the same partner. Explain that they should match the phrases in the top half of the worksheet with the pictures in the bottom half, for example, *a bottle of +* *lemonade.*

4 Check answers in open class.

5 When you have checked all answers, ask half of the students (Student As) to fold their pieces of paper in half once more and look at the pictures in the bottom half. The partners (Student Bs) look at the whole worksheet.

6 Student A looks at each picture and gives a full phrase (*a bottle of lemonade* rather than just *lemonade*) for each picture. Student B checks Student A's answers and gives one point for each correct answer. Students then swap roles. The student with the most correct guesses is the winner.

Follow up

Students can work together to think of other items that can be counted in the same containers (e.g.: *a box of chocolates, a box of matches, a box of tissues* etc.) scoring one point for each correct combination. The pair with the most correct combinations wins.

Answers

a box of chocolates
a carton of milk
a jar of honey
a bottle of lemonade
a packet of crisps
a tin of tuna fish
a can of coke
a loaf of bread
a bowl of fruit
a bar of chocolate

6A *Containers*

a bar of

a packet of

a carton of

a box of

a loaf of

a jar of

a can of

a bottle of

a tin of

a bowl of

FOLD --- FOLD

lemonade

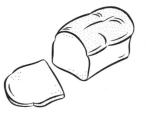

Photocopiable

6B Healthy or hopeless

Sue Kay

Type of activity

Pair work. Reading and speaking.

Aim

To recycle food vocabulary, *how much, how many, a lot* and *not much*.

Task

To interview a partner about their eating habits.

Preparation

Make one copy of the worksheet for each student and cut the copies up as indicated.

Timing

30–40 minutes.

Procedure

1 Ask the students to work in pairs. Give one copy of the questionnaire to each student in the class but do not give out the *What it means* section yet.

2 Give them a few minutes to read the questionnaire and to ask any questions about words they do not know.

3 Now ask them to take it in turns to ask their partner the questions on the questionnaire and to note down their answers.

4 When they have interviewed one another, they should add up their partner's score.

5 Give the *What it Means* section to each pair of students and ask them to read out their partner's results.

Variation

Ask the students to read the questionnaire and answer the questions silently, and then compare results with a partner.

6B *Healthy or hopeless*

QUESTIONNAIRE

Answer the questions to find out how good your diet is.

1 What's your favourite meal?
a Breakfast.
b Lunch.
c Dinner.

2 How many glasses of water do you drink every day?
a One.
b Three.
c Five or more.

3 How much fruit do you eat every day?
a One piece.
b Three pieces.
c Five or more pieces.

4 What's your favourite kind of tea?
a Black.
b Green.
c Herbal.
d I never drink tea.

5 How many cups of coffee do you drink every day?
a One.
b Three.
c Five or more.

6 What do you usually eat for breakfast?
a Fruit.
b Bread.
c Cereal.
d I never eat breakfast.

7 What are your favourite vegetables?
a Green vegetables like beans, cauliflower and lettuce.
b Red vegetables like tomatoes and red peppers.
c Potatoes – preferably chips.

8 How much chocolate do you eat?
a A lot.
b Not much.
c I never eat chocolate.

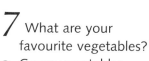

9 What's your favourite bread?
a Brown.
b White.
c I never eat bread.

10 How much sugar do you put in your coffee and tea?
a Two spoons or more.
b One spoon.
c None.
d I never drink coffee or tea.

11 What's your favourite kind of mineral water?
a Still.
b Sparkling.
c I only drink coke.

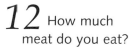

12 How much meat do you eat?
a A lot.
b Not much.
c I never eat meat.

SCORE

1	a 4	b 3	c 2	
2	a 2	b 3	c 4	
3	a 2	b 3	c 4	
4	a 2	b 3	c 4	d 4
5	a 4	b 2	c 0	
6	a 4	b 3	c 3	d 0
7	a 4	b 3	c 1	
8	a 0	b 2	c 4	
9	a 3	b 2	c 2	
10	a 0	b 2	c 3	d 4
11	a 4	b 3	c 0	
12	a 1	b 3	c 4	

✂ ··

What it means ...

You scored 13 to 25
OH DEAR! – You eat too many of the wrong things, and not enough of the right things.

You scored 26 to 35
BALANCED – You eat a good balanced diet but you are not obsessed with food.

You scored 36 or over
HEALTHY – Your diet is very good – are you sure you told the truth?

Photocopiable

7A I'm a model

Nicholas Sheard

Type of activity

Vocabulary and discussion. Writing.

Aim

To revise character adjectives and practise talking about different jobs.

Task

To talk about different jobs and the personal characteristics needed to do them.

Preparation

Make one copy of the worksheet for each student.

Timing

40 minutes.

Procedure

1 Draw pictures or mime some of the jobs mentioned in exercise 1 on the board. Elicit the jobs from the students. Drill and check pronunciation.
2 Give each student a copy of the worksheet. Ask students to read the jobs in exercise 1 and then discuss with a partner. Monitor, helping with vocabulary and pronunciation. Check understanding and drill pronunciation with the whole class.
3 Students do exercise 2 in pairs. Check answers with the whole class.
4 Students do exercises 3 and 4 in pairs. Monitor, helping with vocabulary and pronunciation.
5 Give students five minutes to write their text for exercise 5. Monitor, helping with sentence construction.
6 Ask students to present themselves to their partner. After a few minutes, invite students to mingle with each other introducing themselves and their jobs.

Follow up

Students write a job description for one of the jobs in exercise 1. This description should include the personal characteristics necessary to do the job.

Answers

Exercise 2
a) dentist   b) nanny   c) driving instructor
d) football manager   e) actor

7A *I'm a model*

1 Look at the list of jobs in the box. How many do you know? How do you say them? Discuss with a partner.

> journalist   taxi driver   teacher   vet   brain surgeon   accountant   actor
> driving instructor   pilot   personal assistant   model   radio DJ   dentist
> football manager   hairdresser   factory worker   telesales person   engineer
> nanny   farmer   nurse   politician   research scientist   librarian

2 Match each 'quote' with one of the jobs in exercise 1.
Can you imagine what people doing some of the other jobs might say?

a 'OK Mrs Clark, lie back, open wide, and relax please.'
b 'She had a bottle of milk at 2, and then slept for an hour.'
c 'Turn right at the next junction please.'
d 'I want you to play as a team in the second half, please!'
e 'They were a wonderful audience tonight!'

3 Choose three jobs from exercise 1 that you would like to do,
and three that you wouldn't like to do. Compare with a partner.

4 Look at these adjectives to describe character. Match the characteristics
with the jobs you chose in exercise 3. Discuss your choices with a partner.

> adventurous   ambitious   creative   energetic   hard-working   independent   practical
> romantic   serious   sociable   confident   helpful   kind   honest   cheerful

5 Choose one of the jobs from exercise 1 and imagine that it's your real job.
Prepare to talk about who you are and what you do. Write down two facts
about your job: one positive and one negative thing.

e.g. I'm a model. I love wearing beautiful designer clothes.
But I can't eat food like cakes and chocolate. I don't like this so much!

_____

_____

_____

6 Work in pairs. Use what you have written in exercise 5 to introduce yourself and
your job to your partner and other students in the class.

Photocopiable

7B Hard work

Carmen Santos Maldonado

Type of activity

Reading, listening and speaking. Group work.

Aim

To practise modals of obligation (*can't, have to, don't have to*). To revise vocabulary of character and of jobs.

Task

To play a game where students have to guess a job from some given clues.

Preparation

Make a copy of the worksheet for every group of three or four students and cut the copies up as indicated.

Timing

15–20 minutes.

Procedure

1 Tell your students that they are going to work in groups guessing different jobs from some clues. There will be six clues for each job, the first clue being quite difficult and the last clue being very easy.

2 Demonstrate the activity to the whole class by reading out the clues (below) for the job of a *clown*. Elicit at least two possible jobs after every clue. Explain that as the clues get easier, the right answer is worth fewer points.
First clue:
You are fit and energetic. (6 points)
Second clue:
You have to be confident. (5 points)
Third clue:
You can't look sad. (4 points)
Fourth clue:
You work in a circus. (3 points)
Fifth clue:
You have to make people laugh. (2 points)
Sixth clue:
You wear funny clothes and colours on your face.
(1 point)

3 Divide the class into groups of three or four and give each group a set of cards, which should be shuffled and placed on the desk facing down.

4 Explain the rules of the game:
  • One student in every group picks the top card from the pile and reads out the clues, one at a time.
  • After listening to each clue, the other students in the group should suggest at least two jobs in response to the clue.
  • If the guess is not correct, the first student reads out the next clue, and so on.
  • The person that guesses correctly gets the number of points indicated next to the clue, picks the next card from the pile, and starts reading out the clues, while the other students try to guess.
  • The game finishes when all the cards have been read. The winner is the student with most points.

5 Circulate and check that the students are following the rules properly.

Follow up

As further revision, ask every student to choose one of the cards and to look at the clues again very carefully for two minutes. Then tell them to swap cards and test their partner to see how many clues they can remember.

For homework, ask the students to think of a different job and to write six clues.

7B *Hard work*

Clues

You don't work in an office. *(6 points)*

You have to be fit. *(5 points)*

You can't eat unhealthy food. *(4 points)*

You have to do a lot of training. *(3 points)*

You have to be quite musical. *(2 points)*

You like dancing very much. *(1 point)*

dancer

Clues

You have to be good at talking to people. *(6 points)*

You have to keep your place of work very clean. *(5 points)*

You can't smoke at work. *(4 points)*

You have to be skilful with a knife. *(3 points)*

You are probably not a vegetarian! *(2 points)*

You sell meat to other people. *(1 point)*

butcher

Clues

You have to work outside. *(6 points)*

You don't have to travel very far. *(5 points)*

You work with water. *(4 points)*

You have to use a bucket in your work. *(3 points)*

You can't be afraid of heights. *(2 points)*

You have to clean a lot of windows. *(1 point)*

window cleaner

Clues

You have to be adventurous and helpful. *(6 points)*

You can't be afraid of heights. *(5 points)*

You can't work from home. *(4 points)*

You have to be ready for emergencies. *(3 points)*

You have to wear a uniform and a helmet. *(2 points)*

You have to save people from buildings on fire. *(1 point)*

fireman

Clues

You like History and Geography. *(6 points)*

You don't have to use a computer. *(5 points)*

You have to be sociable and outgoing. *(4 points)*

You don't have to wear a uniform. *(3 points)*

You have to have a clear voice. *(2 points)*

You have to explain things to tourists. *(1 point)*

tourist guide

Clues

You have to like talking to people. *(6 points)*

You have to stand up for a long time. *(5 points)*

You have to be good with your hands. *(4 points)*

You work with mirrors. *(3 points)*

You help people look more attractive. *(2 points)*

You have to cut and comb other people's hair. *(1 point)*

hairdresser

Photocopiable

8A *Summer holiday*

Peter Maggs

Type of activity

Reading and writing. Groupwork.

Aim

To practise *wh-* questions.

Task

To work together to answer some questions and write them in a puzzle.

Preparation

Make one copy of the worksheet for each group of three students in the class and cut into four pieces (one for each student in a group of three and one set of questions for the whole group) as indicated.

Timing

15 minutes.

Procedure

1 Brainstorm what your students know about Australia (famous places, animals etc.). Tell them they are going to read about a holiday to Australia.

2 Explain that the description of the holiday is in three parts. Each student in a group of three will have to read one part and then all three will work together to answer some questions.

3 Divide the class into groups of three. Give each student in the group one part of the worksheet (but keep the questions for now). Tell them they have four minutes to read their part.

4 After four minutes, ask students to turn over their pieces of paper. Give each group one set of questions and ask them to work together in their groups to answer the questions. Encourage students not to look at their pieces of paper unless it is absolutely necessary. Ask students to write their answers in the puzzle. Explain that the first group to find the official stone and animal of Queensland (hidden in the answers) is the winner.

5 After answering all of the questions, students should see the words *sapphire* and *koala*, reading from top to bottom. The winning group is the first to call this out.

6 Check answers in open class.

Follow up

Students can choose some of the questions in the worksheet to interview each other about their last holiday.

Answers

1	Australia	10	crocodile
2	By plane	11	By catamaran
3	camped	12	Will
4	party	13	sharks
5	By four-wheel drive		
6	Scuba diving		
7	scared		
8	sea		
9	Two weeks		

8A *Summer holiday*

1 Read the email and answer the questions.

2 Write the answers in the puzzle to reveal the name of Queensland's official stone and official animal.

1 Where did they go? (9)

2 How did they get there? (2,5)

3 What did they do in the rainforest? (6)

4 What did they have at the end of the holiday? (5)

5 How did they travel around in the first week? (2,4,5,5)

6 What did they spend the second week doing? (5,6)

7 How did Kiera feel? (6)

8 In which unusual place did they ride the horses? (3)

9 How long did the holiday last? (3,5)

10 What type of farm did they visit? (9)

11 How did they get to the Great Barrier Reef? (2,9)

12 Who did Kiera go on holiday with? (4)

13 What fish did they see in the water? (6)

Student A

Read your part of Kiera's email to her friend. Then work with Students B and C to answer the questions.

> Hi Anna
> I'm sorry I haven't been in touch sooner – I've been on holiday. I went to Queensland in Australia with Will. We only stayed for two weeks but we had a fantastic time. We flew to Cairns from London and then we rented a four-wheel drive to travel around in, especially for the rough roads.

Student B

Read your part of Kiera's email to her friend. Then work with Students A and C to answer the questions.

> On the second day we drove up to Cape Tribulation and camped in the rainforest. The next day we went to a crocodile farm and saw lots of huge crocodiles – Will was scared but I enjoyed it. Then we stayed at a ranch. For me the highlight was riding the horses into the sea! Yes, we actually rode the horses as they swam!

Student C

Read your part of Kiera's email to her friend. Then work with Students A and B to answer the questions.

> In the second week, we returned to Cairns and then took a catamaran out to The Great Barrier Reef. We spent the next five days scuba diving in different places. We saw a lot of sharks, Anna. And this time I was scared! At the end of the holiday we all had a party in Cairns. We'll definitely go there again! Love Kiera

Photocopiable

8B *A river poem*

Nicholas Sheard

Type of activity

Reading and discussion. Writing.

Aim

To read a poem in English.

Task

To read and complete a poem.

Preparation

Make one copy of the worksheet for each student and one copy for yourself (enlarged to A3 size if possible, or copied onto an OHT).

Timing

30 minutes.

Procedure

1 Pin your own copy of the worksheet onto the board or project it onto an OHP and ask students to gather round you and look at the picture. Ask students if they have been to a river / the seaside recently, or if they can remember a memorable trip to the river / seaside as a child (or adult). Use the picture to pre-teach the following vocabulary: *mill, valley, hill, foam*.

2 Tell students that they are going to read a poem about a river. Tell them that there will be some words that they don't know in the poem, and that the word order and language in the poem is unusual. Write the first line of the poem on the board: *Dark brown is the river ...* . Explain to students that the word order in normal, non-poetic English would be: *The river is dark brown*. If you like, write this line on the board as well: *Green leaves a-floating / Castles of the foam*. Explain to students that *a-floating* means *are floating*, and that the leaves look like castles as they float down the river.

3 Hand out one copy of the worksheet to each student in the class. Read the words in exercise 1 together with the whole class. Check meaning. Ask students to complete the poem. Monitor, helping with vocabulary if necessary.

4 Ask students to check answers in pairs, then check answers with the whole class. A good way to do this is by reading the poem to the students. You can then ask the students to practise reading the poem out loud themselves.

5 Ask students to do exercises 2 and 3 in pairs or small groups. Tell students that there are not any right or wrong answers to these questions, although the original title of the poem is *Where go the boats?*. Ask them, if possible, to give a reason for their answers. Monitor and help with vocabulary as necessary. Lead a feedback and discussion session with the whole class.

6 Students write their own river / sea poems in pairs or small groups. With less confident students, you may choose to miss this final activity. Do not expect too much from the students! Monitor carefully, helping with vocabulary. When they have finished, ask students to read their poems to the rest of the class.

Answers

Dark brown is the river,
Golden is the **sand**,
It flows along for ever,
With **trees** on either hand.

Green leaves a-floating
Castles of the foam
Boats of mine a-boating –
Where will all come **home**?

On goes the river
And out past the mill,
Away down the valley,
Away down the **hill**.

Away down the river,
A hundred **miles** or more,
Other little **children**
Shall bring my boats ashore.

8B A *river poem*

1 Read the poem and complete it using the words in the box.

trees	children	sand
hill	miles	home

Dark brown is the river,
Golden is the _____ .
It flows along for ever,
With _____ on either hand.

Green leaves a-floating
Castles of the foam
Boats of mine a-boating –
Where will all come _____ ?

On goes the river
And out past the mill,
Away down the valley,
Away down the _____ .

Away down the river,
A hundred _____ or more,
Other little _____
Shall bring my boats ashore.

(by Robert Louis Stevenson)

2 Which of these titles do you think is best for the poem? Can you think of any other possibilities?

Where go the boats?
From the river to the sea
Fishing
The beach
Friends
The river runs deep

3 Discussion.

a Describe the person who is sailing the boats.

b Why is he/she sailing boats on the river?

c Describe the river and the boats.

4 In groups, write your own 'Sea/River' poem. Here are some verbs you could use. Check them in your dictionary.

splash	rain	catch	sink
swim	blow	build	float
dig	laugh	lie	eat

Photocopiable

9A Last summer, I ...

Philip Borrell

Type of activity

Running dictation, followed by grammar focus and speaking.

Aim

To practise asking past simple questions.

Task

To dictate a text to a partner, and then ask and answer past simple questions.

Preparation

Make a copy of the worksheet for each student, and one extra. Cut out the text at the top of the extra worksheet.

Timing

20–30 minutes.

Procedure

1 Write two short sentences on the board and stand with your back to the board. Ask a student to dictate the two sentences on the board to you. As the student dictates, ask for repetition, clarification, spelling, etc. For example: *Wait a moment. What did you say? How do you spell that? What comes after ... ?*

2 Elicit these 'repair' expressions, and write them on the board. Check that students know how to describe various punctuation marks – *full stop, comma, apostrophe*, etc.

3 Stick the text from the top of the extra worksheet onto the wall outside the classroom.

4 Put the students into pairs, with Student A as the 'writer' and Student B as the 'reader'. Explain to the students that the 'readers' will dictate a text to their partner (the 'writer'). Tell them that they must use only English.

5 Ask the 'readers' to stand up, go to the text, read it and then return and dictate it to their partner. Instruct 'readers' to stand about one metre away from their partners as they dictate the text. Explain that they will probably

have to return to the text several times, remembering a short 'chunk' of text each time. Monitor to ensure that only English is used.

6 When the students have finished, the 'readers' can sit with their writing partner to check the writing. After they have checked for a few minutes, give them two copies of the worksheet for the final feedback section.

7 Ask the students to complete the questions using the prompts.

8 Tell the students to ask you their questions about your last holiday. After each answer, they should write notes in the first column of the table.

9 Students then write notes about their own holiday to complete the second column of the table and finally they can ask two other students about their holidays to complete the last two columns.

Follow up

A logical next step is for students to write about their last holiday. You may wish to provide some input for the connecting words *and, but, so* and *because* (examples in dictation text) and encourage students to use them in their own writing.

Answers

1 When did you last go on holiday?
2 Where did you go?
3 Who did you go with?
4 How did you go?
5 Where did you stay?
6 What did you do?
7 Did you enjoy it?

Notes & comments

For stage 5 of the *Procedure* above, you could make a barrier of chairs, tables, etc. in a semi-circle just inside the doorway so that the readers have to stand at the barrier and call out the sentences to the writers. (This can work for up to 30 students.)

9A *Last summer, I ...*

✂ ....

Last summer, I went to Phuket in southern Thailand with my brother, Joe. We travelled by plane and stayed at a guesthouse at Kata Beach for 5 days. Every day, I swam and went jetskiing, but Joe didn't because he can't swim very well. He just sunbathed on the beach and slept! In the evenings, we drank cool drinks and watched the sunset, and then, after dinner, we went dancing at a nightclub. We both thought this holiday was fantastic, so we plan to go back to Phuket next year.

✂ ....

Put the words into the correct order to make the questions for these answers.

1 go when you did last on holiday

When did you last go on holiday?   Last summer.

2 you where go did

_____   Phuket.

3 with who you did go

_____   My brother, Joe.

4 did how go you

_____   By plane.

5 stay you did where

_____   At Kata Beach.

6 you what did do

_____   swam/went jetskiing/sunbathed/slept

7 it you enjoy did

_____   Yes, we did!

Now ask the same questions (1–7) to complete the table.

	Teacher	**You**	**Student 1**	**Student 2**
1				
2				
3				
4				
5				
6				
7				

Photocopiable

9B *I guess ...*

Jon Hird

Type of activity

Class mingle.

Aim

To practise past tense questions and answers.

Task

To complete sentences about classmates' past activities and to ask questions to see if the sentences are true or false.

Preparation

Make one copy of the worksheet for each student.

Timing

20–30 minutes.

Procedure

1   Give one copy of the worksheet to each student. Ask them to guess which of their classmates did each of the activities on the worksheet and then to complete the sentences by writing the names of their classmates in the appropriate spaces, for example, *Junko went to a party last weekend.* Encourage the students to write as many different names as possible.

2   When they have completed all the sentences, the students walk around the class asking and answering questions. For example:
Junko, did you go to a party last weekend?
Yes, I did. / No, I didn't.

3   The students tick their correct guesses and put a cross next to their incorrect guesses.

4   The student with the most correct guesses is the winner.

9B *I guess ...*

Who did these things? Write your classmates' names in the spaces
and then ask questions to check your guesses.

I guess ...

✔ or ✗

_____ went to a [image] last weekend ☐

_____ sent an [image] yesterday. ☐

_____ ate in a [image] last week. ☐

_____ listened to some [image] this morning. ☐

_____ watched [image] last night. ☐

_____ sent a [image] today. ☐

_____ spent a lot of [image] last weekend. ☐

_____ came to school by [image] today. ☐

_____ was late for [image] this week. ☐

_____ did some [image] yesterday. ☐

_____ stayed at [image] last night. ☐

_____ didn't have any [image] this morning. ☐

_____ cooked a [image] last night. ☐

_____ didn't do any [image] last night. ☐

Photocopiable

10 *Matching mingle*

Fernando Martín Pescador

Type of activity

Grammar. Group mingle / Pair work.

Aim

To consolidate the main language areas covered in units 1–9 in *Inside Out* Elementary Student's Book.

Task

To match questions and answers.

Preparation

Make one copy of the worksheet and cut it up as indicated.

Timing

10–15 minutes.

Procedure

1   Divide the class into two teams: Team A and Team B.

2   Give one question card to each student in Team A and one answer card to each student in Team B.

3   Explain that each question has a matching answer. Only one answer is correct for each question. The students should try to find the matching half of their question and answer pair.

4   Ask the teams to stand at opposite sides of the room. When you call out 'Go!', the students should walk towards each other and read out the question or answer on their card.

5   When all the question and answer pairs have been matched (or after 15 minutes), ask students to sit down in their pairs.

6   Ask students to read out their matching question and answer in their pairs. The rest of the class can decide if they are correct.

Follow up

You could ask students to prepare their own matching mingle activity. They can find sentences from the Coursebook, split them into two halves and write each half onto a piece of paper or card. Collect in all the cards, shuffle them and redistribute them to students. They then mingle again to find their matching sentence halves.

10 *Matching mingle*

Question cards	Answer cards
How much water do you drink every day?	Two or three glasses.
How many people live in your house?	Three.
When do you get up?	At half past six.
Can you play the piano?	No, I can't.
Do you like fish?	No, I don't.
Where does your brother live?	In America.
How much does this dress cost?	75 euros.
What did you watch on TV last night?	A wildlife documentary.
Did you go to the cinema last week?	Yes, I did.
Can I borrow your umbrella?	Yes, of course you can.
Are you looking forward to your holiday?	Yes, I am!
How often do you eat chocolate?	About once or twice a week.
What's your favourite colour?	Blue.
How do you feel?	Tired.
Is this your bag?	No, it isn't. Mine is black.
Why are you smiling?	Because I feel happy.
What's your telephone number?	0204 733256
Would you like a sandwich?	No, thank you. I'm not hungry.

Photocopiable

11A *Fashion and style*

Elisa Jiménez Lazcano

Type of activity

Writing/vocabulary practice. Individual work.

Aim

To revise vocabulary related to clothes and accessories and practise using the present continuous.

Task

To match words for clothes and accessories with two pictures (one of a woman and the other of a man).

Preparation

Make one copy of the worksheet for each student.

Timing

20 minutes.

Procedure

1 Explain to the students that they are going to revise and practise vocabulary of clothes and the use of the present continuous.

2 Give out a copy of the worksheet to each student. Allow 1–2 minutes for them to read the instructions.

3 Ask the students to look carefully at the two pictures and then to complete the labels using the words from the boxes below.

4 Go through the answers with the whole class.

5 Ask the students to read the instructions for the second task. Explain to the students that they are going to write sentences describing what other students in the class are wearing, using the vocabulary from the first task and the present continuous.

6 Allow students 5–7 minutes to do this task and then check the answers with the whole class. The students can also compare their answers in pairs.

Follow up

Ask students to work in pairs and take it in turns to describe their own clothes. Remind them that they have to use the present continuous.

Answers

Picture 1

1 hat
2 ring
3 bracelet
4 blouse
5 bag
6 scarf
7 skirt
8 coat
9 boots

Picture 2

10 cap
11 glasses
12 shirt
13 vest
14 jacket
15 belt
16 trousers
17 socks
18 trainers

11A *Fashion and style*

1 Use the words in the boxes to label the two pictures below.

1 _____

2 _____

3 _____

4 _____

5 _____

6 _____

7 _____

8 _____

9 _____

10 _____

11 _____

12 _____

13 _____

14 _____

15 _____

16 _____

17 _____

18 _____

blouse	bag	bracelet	skirt
scarf	boots	hat	coat	ring

belt	socks	jacket	glasses	vest
jeans	trainers	shirt	cap	

2 Write at least five sentences to describe a classmate's clothes. Use the words from exercise 1, the adjectives in the box below and the present continuous.

beautiful	dark	short	long	elegant	trendy	casual	formal	lovely	light

Ana is wearing a beautiful long skirt.

_____

_____

_____

_____

_____

Photocopiable

11B *Match the numbers*

Peter Maggs

Type of activity

Speaking. Pair work and group work.

Aim

To practise saying numbers (13/30, 14/40 etc.).

Task

To play a game of matching pairs (pelmanism).

Preparation

Make one copy of the worksheet for each pair of students (or group of four) and cut the copies up as indicated.

Timing

10 minutes.

Procedure

1 Put students into pairs or small groups (four students divided into two pairs).
2 Give each pair/group a set of cards and tell them to place the cards face down on the table.
3 Demonstrate that the aim of the game is to turn over two cards which have the same number on them. If a student turns over a matching pair, they keep it. If they turn over two different cards, they should return them face down to the same place that they took them from. The idea is to remember the position of the cards.
4 The students begin the game with the first player/pair turning over two cards and reading them aloud. They either keep them or replace them. The next player (or pair of players) then takes a turn, and so on.
5 This continues until all the matching numbers have been found. The winner is the player or pair with the most cards.
6 The game can be repeated as often as necessary.

Follow up

For further practice on the difference between *13* and *30*, *14* and *40* etc., write the numbers up on the board and divide the class into two teams. Call out a number and one student from each team has to run to the board and identify the number you call out. The student who identifies the number correctly earns their team a point. The team with the most points at the end of the game is the winner.

11B *Match the numbers*

40	thirteen	f**i**fte**e**n	**sixty** sixty sixty sixty sixty sixty sixty
thirty	14	30	sI**XTE**En
16	**50**	forty	**60**
fourteen	fifty	15	**13**

Photocopiable

12A Who am I?

Philip Borrell

Type of activity
Speaking. Small groups.

Aim
To practise the use of the forms: *want to, would like to, hope to* and *going to.*

Task
To ask questions to identify the other student.

Preparation
Make one copy of the worksheet for each student. Make one copy of the worksheet for each group of three to four students, and cut the copies up as indicated.

Timing
15–20 minutes.

Procedure
1 Pre-teach the following words: *scientist, millionaire, scholarship, cure, research* and *famous.*
2 Write on the board:
   want to   would like to   hope to   going to
   and give each student a copy of the worksheet.
3 Refer to 'Alexei' on the Worksheet, and tell the students 'You are Alexei.' Elicit sentences, for example:
   I want to be a scientist.
   I would like to be a millionaire.
   I hope to travel a lot.
   I'm going to study in London.
4 Do this once or twice more or until the students understand. Then elicit sentences about some other people on the worksheet.
5 Now, ask the students *Who am I?* and say sentences that match one of the people on the worksheet. For example, if you chose Julia, you would say:
   I want to be a professional tennis player.
   I would like to travel a lot.
   I hope to be a millionaire.
   I'm going to practise every day.
   Say these sentences a few times until someone guesses who it is. Then repeat as necessary.

6 Ask a student to choose a name on the worksheet and say sentences while the other students listen and guess who it is. Repeat as necessary.
7 Now demonstrate the game. Sit at a table with two or three strong students. Ask the other students to gather round and watch.
8 Place a set of cards face down on the table. One student picks up a card and makes sentences about that person. The first of the other students to say who it is wins the card. Then the next player picks up a card and makes sentences, and so on. (If students begin calling out names almost at random, you can say they only have one guess per card).
9 Students play the game in groups of three or four.

Variation
1 Elicit the question forms for the above structures, i.e.:
   Do you want ....?
   Would you like ...?
   Do you hope ...?
   Are you going to ...?
   and write them on the board, along with the short answers. Choose a person from the worksheet and have students ask questions to find out who it is. Repeat as necessary.
2 Demonstrate the game again, this time with students asking questions, in turn, around the table. Note that in this version, a student can only guess who it is after they ask their question.

Notes & comments
The cards are useful in that they provide a ready scoring record as well as a finite end to the activity.

12A *Who am I?*

Alexei be a scientist be a millionaire travel a lot study in London	**Bob** be a scientist be a millionaire travel a lot apply for a scholarship	**Cathy** be a scientist be a millionaire find a cure for cancer study in London	**Dan** be a scientist be a millionaire find a cure for cancer apply for a scholarship
Evan be a scientist do research travel a lot study in London	**Fatima** be a scientist do research travel a lot apply for a scholarship	**Geri** be a scientist do research find a cure for cancer study in London	**Harry** be a scientist do research find a cure for cancer apply for a scholarship
Ingrid be a professional tennis player travel a lot be a millionaire have tennis lessons	**Julia** be a professional tennis player travel a lot be a millionaire practise every day	**Klaus** be a professional tennis player be famous be a millionaire have tennis lessons	**Lee** be a professional tennis player be famous be a millionaire practise every day
Maleeya be a professional tennis player travel a lot win Wimbledon have tennis lessons	**Nancy** be a professional tennis player travel a lot win Wimbledon practise every day	**Oliver** be a professional tennis player be famous win Wimbledon have tennis lessons	**Pablo** be a professional tennis player be famous win Wimbledon practise every day

Photocopiable

12B *Make a sentence with ...*

Philip Borrell

Type of activity

Sentence-generation game. Group work

Aim

To practise making sentences using verb patterns starting with *want to, would like to, hope to,* and *going to.*

Task

To make sentences using the verbs on two cards (pelmanism).

Preparation

Make one copy of the worksheet for each group of three to five students. Cut the copies up as indicated and sort into two piles: A and B.

Timing

10–15 minutes.

Procedure

Version 1

1 Divide the class into groups of three to five students.
2 Demonstrate the activity to the class.
3 Spread out the two sets of cards (A and B) face down on the table of your demonstration group.
4 One student turns over two cards. If they are both A cards, or both B cards, s/he turns them back over, and the next student has a turn.
5 If the two cards are an A card and a B card, the student uses the two verbs to make a sentence.
6 If all the students in the group agree that the grammar and meaning of the sentence is correct, that student keeps the pair.
7 The next student turns over two cards as in step 4 above, and so on.

Version 2

1 Divide the class into groups of three to five students.
2 Put the cards face down in two piles – one for A cards, one for B cards.
3 One student turns over the top card on each pile. The other students take turns to say a sentence using the two verbs shown.
4 The student who turned over the cards judges which of the other students has said the best sentence. S/he awards the pair to that student.
5 The next student turns over the top card on each pile as in step 3, and so on.

Notes & comments

Version 1 is easier as students are more likely to offer assistance to their classmates as they try to produce correct sentences. Therefore, it is probably best to play the two games in the order given.

You may want to provide extra verbs to increase the number of possible verb combinations.

12B *Make a sentence with ...*

A Cards

A	A	A	A
would like to	want to	hope to	be going to

A	A	A	A
would like to	want to	hope to	be going to

B Cards

B	B	B	B
study	be	travel	have

B	B	B	B
play	make	meet	write

Photocopiable

13A *What is it?*

Jon Hird

Type of activity

Guessing game. Pair work.

Aim

To consolidate and further practise language for describing objects.

Task

To guess the identity of an object by asking *Yes/No* questions.

Preparation

Make one copy of the worksheet for each student.

Timing

15–30 minutes.

Procedure

Put the students into pairs and give each student a copy of the worksheet. Explain the rules as follows:

1   Student A chooses an object from the worksheet without telling Student B what it is.

2   Student B asks the *yes/no* questions on the worksheet (in any order) and makes up futher sentences, using these as a guide to try to identify the object. Student A can only answer *Yes, it is./No, it isn't., Yes, it has./No, it hasn't.* or *Yes, you do./No, you don't.* to Student B's questions.

3   If at any time Student B thinks s/he knows what the object is, s/he can make a guess. If correct, s/he gets a point and the round finishes. If not correct, this counts as one question and s/he continues asking more questions.

4   The student who is guessing can ask **a maximum of ten questions**. If after ten questions Student B doesn't know the object, s/he has one final guess at the object. If correct, s/he gets a point. If not correct, then student A gets a point.

5   At the end of the round, the students exchange roles and play again. You could set a time limit or play until the first student reaches, say, five points.

13A *What is it?*

Work in pairs.

Student A: Choose one of the objects below. Don't tell Student B what it is!

Student B: Ask questions to find out Student A's object. Use the language in the box at the bottom of the page. You may ask no more than ten questions.

Student A: Answer Student B's questions. You may answer only *Yes, it is./No, it isn't., Yes, it has./No, it hasn't.* or *Yes, you do./No, you don't.* to Student B's questions.

Is it made of ...	metal / plastic / cloth / paper / glass *etc.* ?
Is it ...	round / square / rectangular / irregular-shaped / long / thin / wide *etc.* ? black / white / grey / silver / multi-coloured *etc.* ?
Is it bigger/smaller than ...	a book / a television / a car *etc.* ?
Has it got ...	buttons / wheels / moving parts *etc.* ?
Do you use it to ...	send messages / open things / play with / travel in / buy things *etc.* ?

Photocopiable

13B *Quiz time*

Jon Hird

Type of activity

Quiz.

Aim

To consolidate and practise comparatives and superlatives.

Task

To complete a quiz by ordering three items according to size etc.

Preparation

Make one copy of the worksheet for each team of two or three students and one copy of the worsheet for each student.

Timing

30 minutes.

Procedure

1   Put the students into teams of two or three and give each team a copy of the worksheet.
2   Allow the students plenty of time to discuss the questions and write their answers. The students only have to write the letters as their answers at this stage.
3   When the teams have completed the quiz, ask them to exchange worksheets with another team for marking and then check the answers with the whole class. Award three points if all three are in the correct order and one point if one is in the correct position. The team with the highest score is the winner.
4   Give out one clean worksheet to each student for their records. Ask them to write out their answers as full sentences, with the comparative and superlative forms, using the example in question 1 as a model, for further practice or for homework.

Answers

  1   b, a, c
  2   c, a, b
  3   a, b, c
  4   a, c, b
  5   c, a, b
  6   b, a, c
  7   a, c, b
  8   b, c, a
  9   b, c, a
10   b, a, c
11   a, b, c
12   c, a, b

13B *Quiz time*

Put the alternatives into the correct order starting with the highest, biggest, most common etc. Question 1 has been done as an example.

1
a **Kilimanjaro**
b **Everest** high
c **Fuji**

Answer B, A, C
Everest is the highest and Kilimanjaro is higher than Mount Fuji

2
a **Amazon**
b **Mississippi** long
c **Nile**

Answer _____

3
a **fear of spiders**
b **fear of flying** common
c **fear of heights**

Answer _____

4
a **cheetah**
b **rabbit** fast
c **horse**

Answer _____

5
a **Mars**
b **Mercury** near to the earth
c **Venus**

Answer _____

6
a **Frankfurt Airport**
b **Heathrow Airport** busy
c **JFK Airport**

Answer _____

7
a **chimpanzee**
b **dolphin** intelligent
c **gorilla**

Answer _____

8
a **Australia**
b **Russia** big
c **Brazil**

Answer _____

9
a **Buddhism**
b **Christianity** popular
c **Islam**

Answer _____

10
a **New York**
b **Tokyo** populous
c **London**

Answer _____

11
a **elephant**
b **rhinoceros** heavy
c **hippopotamus**

Answer _____

12
a **I**
b **it** common in spoken English
c **the**

Answer _____

Photocopiable

14A *What should I do?*

José María Mateo Fernández

Type of activity

Speaking. Whole class mingle.

Aim

To practise vocabulary related to problems and giving advice (*should/shouldn't*).

Task

To guess a situation by using the advice/clues from different classmates.

Preparation

Make one copy of the worksheet and cut it up as indicated.

Make one copy of the worksheet for each student and do not cut it up.

Each student will need one pin.

Timing

15–30 minutes (depending on number of students per class).

Procedure

1   After having cut up all the cards, place them face down on your desk and ask the students to take one each. Make sure they do NOT read them.

2   Pin each student's card onto the back of his/her jacket or shirt.

3   Ask students to walk around, read each other's sentences and respond to other students' cards by giving some advice using *should* or *should't*. For example:
Student A's card reads: *You have just won the lottery. Now you're a millionaire!*
Student B says: *I think you should go out tonight and celebrate.*

4   When all students have talked to everyone else, they should try to guess what is written on their own cards.

5   Give each student a copy of the worksheet and discuss some of the funniest answers/reactions as a whole class.

Follow up

In pairs. Ask students to think of some similar *extreme* situations and write them down on small pieces of paper. Once they have finished, collect them and hand them out to other pairs so that they can give some further advice.

14A *What should I do?*

You're going to join the army tomorrow.	You know your son/daughter has started smoking and s/he's only 14.	You're the only survivor on a desert island.
You have just failed your driving test.	You have a very important exam tomorrow. Your neighbours upstairs are having a party and you can't concentrate.	You're getting married on Sunday, and today is Friday.
You have just won the lottery. Now you're a millionaire!	You're 35 now. You always wanted to be a doctor but your parents made you study engineering.	You hate your nose. You want to have cosmetic surgery on it but you have no money right now.
You borrowed a friend's expensive watch yesterday and now you have lost it.	You take your boyfriend/girlfriend to an expensive restaurant. When the waiter brings the bill, you realize your wallet is still at home.	It's your wedding anniversary today and you have forgotten to buy a present for your wife/husband.

Photocopiable

14B *Character jumble*

Jon Hird

Type of activity

Crossword.

Aim

To consolidate and practise adjectives of character.

Task

To complete a crossword by rearranging the jumbled letters of character adjectives and then to discuss questions about the adjectives.

Preparation

Make one copy of the worksheet for each student.

Timing

20–30 minutes.

Procedure

1 Give one copy of the worksheet to each student and ask them to complete the crossword by rearranging the jumbled letters of character adjectives. You could help the students by telling them that the first and last letter of the mixed-up words are correct. The students can either do the crossword individually or working together in pairs. You could add a competitive element by making the first student or team to finish the winner.

2 When the students have finished the crossword, check the answers and meaning with the class.

3 The students then work in pairs or small groups to discuss the questions in exercise 2.

4 Go through students' answers to exercise 2 with the whole class.

Answers

1

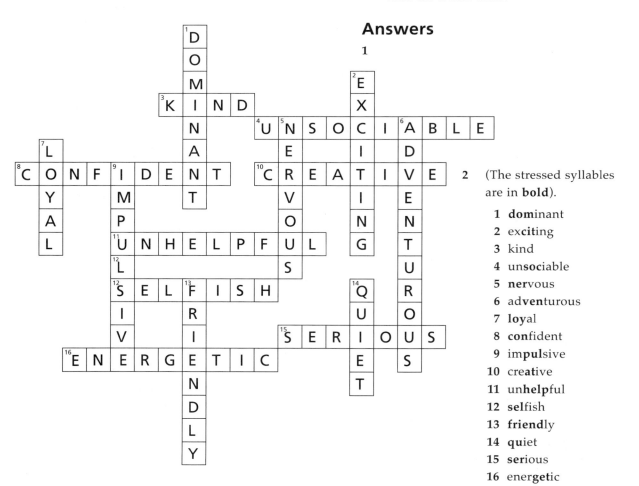

2 (The stressed syllables are in **bold**).

1 **dom**inant
2 ex**cit**ing
3 **kind**
4 un**so**ciable
5 **ner**vous
6 ad**ven**turous
7 **loy**al
8 **con**fident
9 im**pul**sive
10 cre**a**tive
11 un**help**ful
12 **sel**fish
13 **friend**ly
14 **quiet**
15 **ser**ious
16 ener**get**ic

14B *Character jumble*

1 Complete the crossword by rearranging the jumbled character adjectives.

Across

3 knid
4 unabsoclie
8 codnenfit
10 creviate
11 unfulphel
12 seslfih
15 seuiros
16 enterigec

Down

1 donnimat
2 exnictig
5 neovrus
6 aderuvontus
7 laoyl
9 imuvlipse
13 frednily
14 qeuit

2 Work in pairs and for each of the adjectives:

a decide which is the stressed syllable.

b decide whether it has positive, negative or neutral meaning.

c think of a person, either famous or someone you know, who can be described using the adjective.

Photocopiable

15 Silly mistakes

Jon Hird

Type of activity

Error correction and discussion.

Aim

To consolidate and further practise the main language areas covered in units 11 to 14 of *Inside Out* Elementary Student's Book.

Task

To correct mistakes in fourteen sentences and then to use these sentences for discussion.

Preparation

Make one copy of the worksheet for each student.

Timing

20–30 minutes.

Procedure

1   Give a worksheet to each student. Tell the students that each sentence contains a mistake. Ask the students, working individually or together in pairs, to find the mistakes and correct them. They should write the corrections on the worksheet.

2   When they have corrected all the sentences, or corrected as many as they can, ask them to compare their corrections with another student if they originally worked individually, or with another pair if they originally worked in pairs.

3   Check the answers with the whole class. Be prepared to refer back to units 11 to 14 of *Inside Out* Elementary Student's Book as necessary.

4   Ask the students, working in pairs or small groups, to discuss the questions. Encourage them to ask follow-up questions to develop the discussions. Refer them to the example questions on the worksheet.

5   When the discussions have finished, ask each student to tell the class one interesting piece of information they have learned about their partner(s).

Answers

1   When do you usually listen <u>to</u> music?
2   What kind <u>of</u> mobile phone have you got?
3   Are you <u>reading</u> a book at the moment?
4   Would you like <u>to</u> live in a foreign country one day?
5   Do you speak English better <u>than</u> your parents?
6   How many times <u>a</u> week do you have an English lesson?
7   Have we got <u>enough eggs</u> to make a cake?
8   How often <u>do you send</u> emails?
9   What <u>are</u> you going to do at the weekend?
10 Do you sometimes <u>have too much homework</u>?
11 Where do you hope <u>to</u> go for your next holiday?
12 <u>What</u> is your favourite colour?
13 Which is <u>the</u> best football team in your country?
14 <u>Are</u> you having a good time today?

15 *Silly mistakes*

1 Each sentence contains a mistake. Find the mistakes and correct them.
The first one has been done for you.

1   When do you usually listen music?
                                   to

2   What kind mobile phone have you got?

3   Are you read a book at the moment?

4   Would you like live in a foreign country one day?

5   Do you speak English better as your parents?

6   How many times week do you have an English lesson?

7   Have we got eggs enough to make a cake?

8   How often send you emails?

9   What you going to do at the weekend?

10   Do you sometimes too much homework have?

11   Where do you hope go for your next holiday?

12   How is your favourite colour?

13   Which is most best football team in your country?

14   Do you having a good time today?

2 In pairs or small groups, ask and answer the questions.
Ask further questions to find out more information:

When do you usually listen to music?

What kinds of music do you listen to?

Have you got a favourite group or singer?

Photocopiable

16A *The internet and me*

Philip Borrell

Type of activity

Running dictation, followed by question and answer session.

Aim

To practise present perfect questions about the internet.

Task

To dictate a text to a partner, and then ask and answer questions in groups.

Preparation

Make one copy of the worksheet for each student, and one extra. Cut out the text at the top of the extra worksheet.

Timing

25–35 minutes.

Procedure

1 Write two short sentences on the board, and stand with your back to the board. Ask a student to dictate the two sentences on the board to you. As the student dictates, ask for repetition, clarification, spelling, etc. For example: *Wait a moment. What did you say? How do you spell that? What comes after …?*

2 Elicit these 'repair' expressions, and write them on the board. Check that students know how to describe various punctuation marks – *full stop, comma, apostrophe,* etc.

3 Stick the text from the top of the extra worksheet onto the wall outside the classroom.

4 Put the students into pairs, with Student A as the 'writer' and Student B as the 'reader'. Explain to the students that the 'readers' will dictate a text to their partner (the 'writer'). Tell them that they must use only English.

5 Ask the 'readers' to stand up, go to the text, read it and then return and dictate it to their partner. Instruct 'readers' to stand about one metre away from their partners as they dictate the text. Explain that they will probably have to return to the text several times, remembering a short 'chunk' of text each time. Monitor to ensure that only English is used.

6 When the students have finished, the 'readers' can sit with their writing partner to check the writing. After they have checked for a few minutes, give them two copies of the worksheet for the final feedback section.

7 Ask the students to use their information about Anthony to complete the first column of the table.

8 Check the answers in open class.

9 Divide the students into groups of three. Tell them to ask and answer the questions in the table, and write notes.

10 Circulate as students are asking and answering their questions, monitoring the activity and helping with any queries.

Notes & comments

At this level, the present perfect questions are the main aim of the activity. However, encourage students to ask more questions if they can.

16A *The internet and me*

> **Anthony**
>
> Yes, I've surfed the internet, many times. I haven't been in a chat room, so, obviously, I've never met anyone from a chat room. Have I used a search engine? Well, yes, I have. I use Google or Yahoo search engines quite often. Last week I had to find out about the Kalahari desert, and I got the information from the internet. I bought something through the internet once. It was a book on geology. Have I ever bought pirated software? Of course not!

Write notes in the table about Anthony.

Have you ever ...	Anthony	Student 1	Student 2
... surfed the internet?			
... been in a chat room?			
... met anyone from a chat room?			
... used a search engine?			
... used the internet to find information?			
... bought something through the internet?			
... bought pirated software?			
... been to an internet café?			
... sent an email to someone in the USA?			
... played an on-line computer game?			
... downloaded music from a music website?			

Now ask your classmates questions and write notes in the table about them.

Photocopiable

16B Have you ever *bingo*

Jon Hird

Type of activity

Class mingle, asking and answering questions.

Aim

To consolidate and practise present perfect + *ever*.

Task

To complete a bingo card with students' names by asking questions.

Preparation

Make one copy of the worksheet per six students in the class and cut it up as indicated.

Timing

20–30 minutes.

Procedure

1 Pre teach the following vocabulary from the bingo cards: *bungee jump, credit card, trophy, drums, octopus, wallet, accident, celebrity, ID card, x-ray, tattoo, operation, break your leg, fall in love.*

2 Give out one bingo card to each student. Explain that the aim of the game is to complete the bingo card with the names of students who have ever done the activities on their card.

3 Remind students how to form the present perfect with *ever* and revise the irregular past participles: *done, been, gone, broken, had, lost, won, eaten, found, met, fallen, seen, ridden.*

4 Tell students to walk around the class asking their classmates in turn *Have you ever ...?* questions about the activities on their card, for example: *Have you ever visited New York? Have you ever done a bungee jump?* When a student answers *yes* to a question, his/her name is written in pencil next to the activity. Once the card is complete, with a name written in for each of the activities, the student should shout *Bingo!* If no-one in the class can answer *yes* to a question, the student can complete his/her card by writing *no-one* in the space. The first student to call out *Bingo!* is the winner.

5 Ask the students to rub out the names, exchange their bingo cards and play the game again. Alternatively you may want to give out fresh bingo cards. Repeat this as many times as you feel is appropriate.

16B Have you ever *bingo*

visit New York	do a bungee jump
break a leg	play the piano
lose a credit card	win a trophy

visit Australia	go surfing
have toothache	play the drums
eat octopus	find a wallet

visit London	go fishing
have an accident	play the guitar
meet a celebrity	lose your ID card

visit Paris	climb a mountain
have an x-ray	play golf
be on TV	fall in love

visit Russia	go scuba diving
have a tattoo	play basketball
ride a motorbike	break the law

visit Egypt	go skiing
break your arm	see a whale
win some money	have an operation

Photocopiable

17A *Circuit training*

Fernando Alba

Type of activity

Revision game. Four teams competing and moving about.

Aim

To revise and practise structures, vocabulary and pronunciation introduced in *Inside Out* Elementary Student's Book.

Task

To work in groups and complete a worksheet.

Preparation

Make four copies of the worksheet and cut the copies up as indicated.

Make one copy of the key for each student for the final feedback part of the activity.

Provide four English dictionaries for the final part of the activity.

Timing

40–50 minutes.

Procedure

1   Stick one of the photocopied activities: *Grammar, English in Use, Pronunciation* and *Vocabulary* on the wall in each corner of the classroom.

2   Divide the class into four teams and ask them to choose a name for their team. Tell students that they should try to complete the task in each corner of the classroom in their teams. They must remember to write their team name at the top of the task sheet.

3   They will have eight minutes per task. At the end of the eight minutes, you will collect in the completed tasks and stick up a new blank task sheet. Each team will then move on to a different corner of the classroom.

4   Once all the teams have completed all four tasks, tell students to sit down in their teams. Give each team a copy of the key, an English dictionary and another team's task sheets to mark.

5   Circulate, while students are marking the sheets, checking that they are marking fairly and dealing with any language queries.

6   Return the marked task sheets to the original teams and find out which group has the highest score.

Answers

Grammar

1   She is a <u>very intelligent</u> woman.
2   Mary <u>always</u> has ~~the~~ dinner at 8 p.m.
3   After dinner he <u>saw</u> a film on TV last night.
4   David always <u>cooks</u> and Phillipa does the <u>washing up</u>.
5   My mother gets to <u>work</u> at ~~the~~ 9.30 a.m.
6   He has ~~the~~ toast and coffee <u>for breakfast</u> every day.
7   Where <u>are you going / are you going to go</u> on holiday next summer?
8   I <u>would like/'d like</u> to buy <u>some / a pair of</u> jeans tomorrow.

Vocabulary

Use your dictionaries to check the answers. One point for every correct word.

Pronunciation

/ʌ/	much	but	cut	son
/ɜː/	word	girl	first	work
/ɔː/	more	four	walk	door
/iː/	easy	meet	three	seat
/ɪ/	big	ship	rich	bit

English in use

1 h   2 e   3 f   4 b   5 i
6 j   7 a   8 c   9 d   10 g

17A *Circuit training*

Grammar

Team _____

Read the sentences below and correct the mistakes.

1 She is a woman very intelligent.

   _____

2 Mary has the dinner at 8 p.m. always.

   _____

3 After dinner he see a film in TV last night.

   _____

4 David always cook and Phillipa does the wash up.

   _____

5 My mother gets to job at the 9.30 a.m.

   _____

6 He has for breakfast the toast and coffee every day.

   _____

7 Where you go on holiday next summer?

   _____

8 I like to buy a jeans tomorrow.

   _____

Vocabulary

Team _____

Write as many words as possible related to these topics.

Things in the kitchen
Vegetables and fruit
Parts of the body

Pronunciation

Team _____

Match the words with the same vowel sounds and put them into the correct box.

more word easy much four big
ship walk rich meet girl but three
first work seat door cut bit son

/ʌ/ e.g. come	/ɜː/ e.g. bird	/ɔː/ e.g. draw

/iː/ e.g. cheap	/ɪ/ e.g. trip

English in use

Team _____

Match each sentence with the best response. Use each response once only.

Sentence	Response
1 Have a nice weekend.	a) How do you do.
2 What does he look like?	b) Here you are.
3 How are you?	c) What a pity!
4 I haven't got a pen.	d) I'm a waiter.
5 Italian food is the best.	e) He's very thin.
6 Where are you from?	f) Fine, thanks.
7 How do you do?	g) He's a nice boy
8 I can't come tonight.	h) Thanks. You too.
9 What do you do?	i) Do you think so?
10 What's he like?	j) Italy.

1 ____ 2 ____ 3 ____ 4 ____ 5 ____

6 ____ 7 ____ 8 ____ 9 ____ 10 ____

Photocopiable

17B *It takes ages!*

Philip Borrell

Type of activity
Vocabulary match. / Whole-class speaking.

Aim
To practise questions about transport to work or school.

Task
To mill around the classroom, asking and answering questions.

Preparation
Make one copy of the worksheet for each student.

Timing
15–20 minutes.

Procedure
1 Ask the students to match the expressions at the top of the page – one has been done as an example.
2 Ask the students to fill in the table – you may want to do the first line as an example. Then ask the students to complete the bottom line about themselves.
3 Refer to the table at the bottom of the page. Elicit and drill the three questions.
4 Ask the students to mill around the class, asking and answering the questions, and then complete the table.

Follow up
You can use the students' completed tables to lead into a writing activity in which students write about how they and their classmates come to school / go to work (using the connectors *and* and *but*).

Notes & comments
This activity may be best used as a warmer / lead-in to the unit.

Answers

	Type of transport	Leave home	Arrive	How long does it take?
Ann	bus	8:10	8:55	*45 minutes*
Ben	car / ferry	7:30	*9:00*	90 minutes
Chris	foot / train	*7:45*	8:45	one hour

17B *It takes ages!*

1 Draw lines to match the words in the two columns.

I go by car.	I walk by the canal.
I go by taxi.	I catch the 7.20 from platform 7.
I go on foot.	I ride my Kawasaki 600.
I go by bus.	I catch a cab.
I go by train.	I drive along the motorway.
I go by ferry.	I catch the number 49. It goes down the High Street.
I go by motorbike.	I take the 7.15 boat from Liberty Harbour.

2 Complete this table.

Name	Type of transport	Leave home	Arrive	How long does it take?
Ann	bus	8:10	8:55	_____
Ben	car / ferry	7:30	_____	90 minutes
Chris	foot / train	_____	8:45	one hour
You	_____	_____	_____	_____

3 Now ask your classmates how they come school or go to work.
Complete the table.

Name	Transport	How long ... ?

Photocopiable

18A *How do you do it?*

Peter Maggs

Type of activity

Grammar. Team game.

Aim

To practise adverbs of manner.

Task

To mime an action to a group who try to guess the action and the adverb of manner.

Preparation

Make one copy of the worksheet and cut it up as indicated.

Timing

10–15 minutes.

Procedure

1   Divide the class into two groups. Tell them they are going to play a game against each other.

2   Explain that you are going to mime an action and they should call out what it is. Explain that the answer ends in an adverb of manner. Mime an action of your own choice (*Make a cup of tea quickly, brush your teeth slowly* etc.) making sure your students understand that they have to guess both the action and the adverb of manner.

3   Tell each team to take it in turns to send one player to the front of the class. The player picks up one of the mime cards and reads the sentence. The player then has 30 seconds to mime the action on the card while their team calls out guesses. If the mime has not been guessed after 30 seconds, the other team can steal a point by giving the correct answer. Each team then takes it in turns to guess the answer until one team gets it right. Teams can score one point for a correct action and one point for a correct adverb of manner. Any team guessing both a correct action and adverb immediately, score four points.

4   The game continues until all the cards are used up. The team that has the most points at the end is the winner.

Follow up

Students can make their own cards for the teacher to store and use at a later date as a warmer or five-minute filler.

Notes & comments

The game can also be played in pairs. Each player has half the cards. Students take it in turns to mime to each other; if their partner guesses correctly, they get the card. The winner is the player with the most cards at the end. The game can also be played in small groups (of five) with two pairs playing against each other while the fifth person is referee.

18A *How do you do it?*

Get dressed
quickly

Play the
drums loudly

Do the ironing
angrily

Write your name
beautifully

Do your homework
happily

Drive the car
carefully

Play tennis
badly

Arrive for the
lesson late

Play the guitar
badly

Eat a banana
slowly

Do the washing up
unhappily

Play the piano
quietly

Photocopiable

18B Telling tales

José María Mateo Fernández

Type of activity

Jigsaw reading. Riddle.

Aim

To practise reading skills and to use time adverbials in context.

Task

To put the different parts of a story into the correct order.

To create an ending for the story.

Preparation

Make one copy of the worksheet for each student. Cut up the copies as indicated and shuffle the pieces.

Timing

20–30 minutes.

Procedure

1 Pre-teach the following vocabulary: *chew, plant* (v), *merchant, qualities, instructions, worried, satisfied, impressed, to make excuses for someone.*

2 Divide the class into groups of three or four.

3 Explain to the students that they are going to read an Indian folk tale, which is also a riddle. They will have to put the different parts of the story into the correct order and then try to solve the riddle.

4 Give one set of shuffled pieces to each student.

5 Tell students, in their groups, to put the different parts of the story into the correct order. Once they think they have ordered the story correctly, they should try to fill the gaps with the time adverbials given at the top of the worksheet. Set an eight-minute time limit for this activity.

6 Once the first group has finished, tell everyone else to stop and check answers with the class. Explain any unknown vocabulary.

7 Students get back into their groups again to think of an imaginative solution to the riddle. After a few minutes, check their suggestions and provide them with the solution if necessary.

Follow up

You may want to change the activity slightly by not providing the name of the tale. Ask students to think of an appropriate title after they have ordered the text.

Answer

1 H
2 B (One day)
3 C
4 G (Finally)
5 A
6 D (That evening)
7 F (A few minutes later)
8 E

Solution to the riddle: a watermelon.

18B *Telling tales*

1 Put the different parts of this folk tale into the correct order.
2 Use the time adverbials below to fill the gaps.
3 Can you guess what the boy bought? Discuss your ideas together.

> **a few minutes later**   **finally**   **one day**   **that evening**
> **once upon a time**

All for a Pànsa (An Indian Folk Tale)

A
'Give him this small coin, this pạnsa. Tell him to go to the market, and to buy one thing with this one pạnsa. It must be something to eat, something to drink, something to chew on, something to plant in the garden, and some food for the cow.'

B
_____ when the boy was about 20, his mother asked the merchant to look for a good wife for their son. The merchant believed his lazy son would never get married. But the mother was sure that they could find him a wife.

C
She said, 'He is unusual and intelligent.' She said, 'I know that a good woman will understand his special qualities.' When she spoke like this the merchant got angry.

D
_____ the mother gave the boy the instructions and the one pạnsa coin. The boy started to walk to the market. As he walked, he thought about the problem and became very worried. 'What can I buy for only one pansa?' he asked himself. 'This task is impossible!' He stopped by a river and sat down.

E
'Buy a **** with one pạnsa. Give it to your parents and they will be satisfied.'
The boy followed her instructions. His parents were very impressed and they invited the girl's family to their house for dinner. And so this beautiful, clever girl married the merchant's son; the boy learnt to work hard and they all lived happily ever after.

F
_____ a beautiful girl walked past the river. She saw the boy's sad face and asked him, 'Why are you so unhappy?' He told her everything. 'I know what you can do,' she said.

G
_____ , the merchant said to his wife, 'I have heard these things many times before, but I do not believe you. You love him too much. But, to make you happy, I will give my son one final chance.'

H
Once upon a time a rich merchant lived in a small town. He had one very lazy son and this made the merchant feel very unhappy. But the merchant's wife believed that the son was wonderful and she always made excuses for him.

Photocopiable

19A *Find someone*

Peter Maggs

Type of activity

Grammar. Group mingle/Pair work.

Aim

To practise making questions using the passive.

Task

To make some questions and then ask other students in the class to answer them.

Preparation

Make one copy of the worksheet for each student.

Timing

20 minutes.

Procedure

1 Give one copy of the worksheet to each student in the class.
2 Ask students to work in pairs. Explain that they should make questions from the picture and verb prompts given.
3 When all students have prepared the questions, ask them to stand up and ask their questions to other students in the class. Make it clear that they should only ask one question to one person (not all questions to one person) and write the name of that person in the middle column each time. Depending on the answer, they should tick either *Yes* or *No* in the right-hand column.
4 When all the questions have been answered (or after 15 minutes), ask students to sit down.
5 Ask students report their findings back to the class. (*Silvia wasn't woken up by an alarm clock today. Marco has had two teeth taken out* etc.)

Follow up

You could ask students to write some of their findings up as homework.

Suggested questions

1 Were you woken up by an alarm clock today?
2 Have you ever had a tooth taken out?
3 Were you given a nice present last Christmas?
4 Have you been told off by the teacher this week?
5 Was your watch made in Japan?
6 Have you had your hair cut this month?
7 Are your clothes designed by anyone famous?
8 Has your bicycle ever been stolen?

Notes & comments

This activity could be a sit-down pairwork activity rather than a class mingle. Students prepare the questions and then take it in turns to ask each other, ticking the right-hand column only.

19A *Find someone*

1 Make questions from the prompts below.

2 Move around the class asking the questions to complete the chart.
You must not write the same name twice.

	Name	Yes	No
1 Were you (wake up) by 🕐 today?	_____	☐	☐
2 Have you ever had 😬 (take out)	_____	☐	☐
3 Were you (give) a nice 🎁 last Christmas?	_____	☐	☐
4 Have you been (tell off) by 👨‍🏫 this week?	_____	☐	☐
5 Was your ⌚ (make) in Japan?	_____	☐	☐
6 Have you had your ✂️ (cut) this month?	_____	☐	☐
7 Are your 👡 (design) by anyone famous?	_____	☐	☐
8 Has your 🚲 ever been (steal)?	_____	☐	☐

3 Report your findings back to the class.
Maria was woken up by an alarm clock today.

Photocopiable

19B *Weather forecast*

Nicholas Sheard

Type of activity

Speaking – giving a mini-presentation.

Aim

To practise using *will* and *might*.

Task

To present a weather forecast.

Preparation

Make one copy of the worksheet for each pair of students in the class. Cut out picture slides where indicated.

Timing

40 minutes.

Procedure

1   Tell students that they are going to practise talking about the weather in this lesson.
2   Hand out one copy of the worksheet to each pair of students in the class. Ask students to do exercises 1 and 2 in pairs. Check answers with the whole class.
3   Give students five minutes to read the weather forecast in exercise 3 and to identify which of the picture slides it refers to. Monitor, helping with vocabulary if necessary. Encourage those students who finish quickly to practise reading the forecast out aloud. As an alternative, you could read the forecast to the students yourself, and ask them to identify which of the picture slides it refers to.
4   Ask students in each pair to choose one of the remaining picture slides (B or C) and to prepare a weather forecast to describe it. Tell students to use the forecast in exercise 3 as a model. Less confident students could work together to produce their forecast. More confident students could write their own individual forecast.
6   Students practise and then present their forecasts to their partner / other pairs / other students in the class.

Follow up

1   Students cut up the weather slides and use the individual pictures to put on a map and prepare their own 'tv' weather forecast, which you could record and play back if you have video facilities available.
2   Students look on the internet for weather forecasts in English from different parts of the world. Students compile a list of words and expressions that are used to talk about or describe the weather. http://www.met-office.gov.uk/ is one site to look at.

Answers

1   warm, wet, chilly, bad, cold, dry, fine, good, hot, lovely, mild, unsettled
2   cloudy, foggy, sunny, windy, rainy, snowy, stormy
3   Slide A

19B *Weather forecast*

1 Find 12 adjectives used to describe the weather in this word snake and write them below.

warmwetchillybadcolddryfinegoodhotlovelymildunsettled

_____	_____	_____	_____
_____	_____	_____	_____
_____	_____	_____	_____

2 Now complete these adjectives also used to describe the weather.

clo_ _y   f_g_ _   su_n_   w_nd_   r_i_y   sn_ _y   st_r_y

3 Read this weather forecast. Which of the picture slides below does it describe? Look in your dictionary or ask your teacher about any new words.

> Today will start off foggy and cold with temperatures of about 5 degrees Celsius. A light wind will clear the fog, but it will stay cloudy and cold all afternoon. There will probably be some rain, which may be heavy in some places. The rain will eventually clear and the early evening will be dry and sunny for most of us.

4 Choose one of the other picture slides and write your own weather forecast to describe it. Then practise presenting your forecast to other students in the class.

Photocopiable

20 Jeopardy

Fernando Alba

Type of activity

General revision. Team work.

Aim

To consolidate some of the grammar, vocabulary and pronunciation covered in *Inside Out* Elementary Student's Book.

Task

To choose and answer a variety of questions covering grammar, vocabulary, pronunciation and speaking skills.

Preparation

Make two copies of the worksheet and cut one of the copies up as indicated.

Timing

30–40 minutes.

Procedure

1 Place the worksheet which has not been cut up, face up on your desk. Arrange the cards face down on top of the worksheet, so that you are using the worksheet as a grid.

2 Divide the class into two teams. Explain the rules of the game:

- Students have to answer questions and win points for their team.
- There are four categories of questions, and four difficulty levels for each category. The more difficult the question, the more points the team can win.
- Teams take it in turns, one student at a time, to choose a category and a difficulty level for their question.
- If the question they have chosen has already been answered, they must choose a different category or difficulty level.
- If they answer the question correctly, the team is awarded the card and the number of points written on the card.
- The winning team is the one with the most points at the end of the game.

3 Play the game. For each question, copy the text onto the board so that the whole class can read it.

Follow up

If students enjoyed the game and if time allows, the teams could prepare revision questions for one another using the same categories.

Answers

Vocabulary
75 points:
strong – weak
nephew – niece
near – far
like – hate / dislike
go to sleep – wake up

Grammar

25 points:	50 points:
child – children	**Countable**
family – families	lemon, carrot, grape,
wife – wives	potato, egg
church – churches	**Uncountable**
bus – buses	bread, pasta, meat,
	rice, oil

75 points:

go – went	sleep – slept
hear – heard	can – could
say – said	fly – flew
buy – bought	see – saw

100 points:
unhappy – unhappily
quick – quickly
careful – carefully
good – well
early – early
loud – loudly

Pronunciation
50 points:
cor<u>rect</u>   Chin<u>ese</u>   <u>chi</u>ldren   <u>v</u>isit   <u>in</u>teresting
75 points:
  /s/   envelopes, stamps
  /z/   roads
  /ɪz/ pages, horses
100 points:
  /d/   enjoyed
  /t/   washed
  /ɪd/ divided, needed, created

20 *Jeopardy*

Vocabulary	Grammar	Pronunciation	Speaking

25 points VOCAB

Say these times in English:

08:40 21:30
17:15 10:45
06:05

25 points GRAM

Write the plurals of these nouns.

child
family
wife
church
bus

25 points PRON

Say these words with the correct pronunciation.

afternoon
thirteen
to live
interesting
hotel

25 points SPEAK

Talk non-stop for 30 seconds about your …

routine.

---

50 points VOCAB

Write on the board:

10 types of food
and
10 types of drink

50 points GRAM

Divide the words into *countable* and *uncountable* nouns.

lemon potato
bread egg
pasta meat
carrot rice
grape oil

50 points PRON

Underline the stressed syllable for each word.

correct
Chinese
children
visit
interesting

50 points SPEAK

Talk non-stop for 45 seconds about your …

family.

---

75 points VOCAB

Give the opposite of these words:

strong
nephew
like
near
go to sleep

75 points GRAM

Write the past simple form of these irregular verbs.

go sleep
hear can
say fly
buy see

75 points PRON

Put these words into the correct column.

/s/ /z/ /iz/

pages envelope
roads stamps
horses

75 points SPEAK

Talk non-stop for one minute about your …

free time.

---

100 points VOCAB

Write on the board:

10 items of men's clothes
and
10 items of women's clothes

100 points GRAM

Change these adjectives to adverbs.

unhappy
quick
careful
good
early
loud

75 points PRON

Put these words into the correct column.

/d/ /t/ /ɪd/

divided enjoyed
needed washed
created

100 points SPEAK

Talk non-stop for one and a half minutes about your …

house.